Bartolomé de las Casas

An Account, Much Abbreviated, of the
Destruction of the Indies

With Related Texts

Bartolomé de las Casas

An Account, Much Abbreviated, of the
Destruction of the Indies

With Related Texts

Translated by
Andrew Hurley

Edited, with an Introduction by
Franklin W. Knight

Hackett Publishing Company, Inc.
Indianapolis/Cambridge

For further information, please address:

Hackett Publishing Company, Inc.
P.O. Box 44937
Indianapolis, IN 46244-0937
www.hackettpublishing.com

The 16-century Theodor de Bry engravings that appear on the cover and throughout this work have been provided courtesy of the John Carter Brown Library at Brown University.

The map of the Indies in Las Casas' time (pp. viii–ix) drawn by Helen H. Donovan.

Cover design by Abigail Coyle
Text design by Jennifer Plumley
Composition by Professional Book Compositors, Inc.
Printed at Malloy, Inc.

Library of Congress Cataloging-in-Publication Data

Casas, Bartolomé de las, 1474–1566.
    [Brevísima relación de las destrucción de las Indias. English]
    An account, much abbreviated, of the destruction of the Indies / Bartolomé de las Casas; translated and with a note on the translation by Andrew Hurly; with an introduction by Franklin W. Knight.
        p. cm.
    Includes bibliographical references and index.
    Contents: The laws of Burgos—New laws of the Indies—A treatise on the just causes for war against the Indians—The true history of the Conquest of Mexico / by Bernal Díaz del Castillo—Cartas de relación / from Hernán Cortés.
    ISBN 0-87220-626-2 (cloth) — ISBN 0-87220-625-4 (pbk.)
    1. Indians, Treatment of—Latin America. 2. Spain—Colonies—America. 3. Mexico—History—Conquest, 1519–1540. 4. Casas Bartolomâ de las, 1474–1566. I. Hurley, Andrew. II. Title.
F1411.C31513 2003
323.1'198'009031—dc21   2003047179

ISBN-13: 978-0-87220-626-7 (cloth)
ISBN-13: 978-0-87220-625-0 (pbk.)

The paper used in this publication meets the minimum requirements of American National Standard for Information Sciences—Permanence of Paper for Printed Library Materials, ANSI Z39.48–1984

∞

Contents

Acknowledgments

The editor expresses his gratitude to Professor Sir Roy Augier, who as a teacher, exemplar, and friend has shaped this work in surprising ways; to the late Professor John Phelan, whose long discussions on Las Casas and Sepúlveda continue to resonate; and to Father Stafford Poole, whose insightful observations and material contributions significantly improved the introductory essay.

The translator wishes to thank David Frye for his many generous and accurate suggestions for notes to the text of *Brevísima Relación*, some of which were incorporated just as Professor Frye wrote them.

THE INDIES
IN LAS CASAS' TIME

NEW SPAIN

FL

Caonao

Sancti Spiritu

Mexico City

Tlaxcala

Bay of Campeche

YUCATÁN

Oaxaca

Ciudad Real de Chiapa

GUATINALA

Gulf of Honduras

VICE

Gulf of Tehuantepec

HONDURAS

NICARAGUA

Lake of Nicaragua

Gulf of the Mosquitos

Puerto Plata

La Vega

Boyá

Gul of

Panà

HAITI

Azua Sto. Domingo

Higüey

Lake of Enriquillo

S. Booruco

Enriquillo

I. de la Tortuga

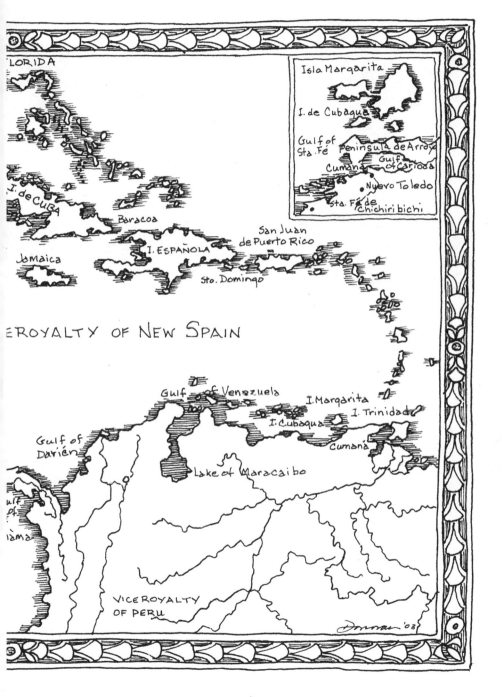

FLORIDA

Isla Marqarita

I. de Cubaqua

Gulf of
Sta.Fé   Peninsula de Arroy

Cumaná   Gulf
of Carioca

I. de CUBA

Nuevo Toledo

Baracoa

Sta. Fé de
Chichiribichi

San Juan
de Puerto Rico

Jamaica

I. ESPAÑOLA

Sto. Domingo

VICEROYALTY OF NEW SPAIN

Gulf of Venezuela

I. Marqarita

I. Trinidad

I. Cubaqua

Gulf of
Darién

Cumaná

Lake of Maracaibo

ulf
of
iamá

VICEROYALTY
OF PERU

Introduction

Dubbed "Protector of the Indians" by Spain's Cardinal Francisco Jiménez de Cisneros only twenty-four years after Columbus first reached the New World, Bartolomé de las Casas emerged in his own lifetime as one of the most important and controversial figures of the early-modern encounter between Europeans and Native Americans.[1] Born possibly as early as 1474 (but probably in 1484), Las Casas lived in an age of remarkable people—yet stood out like a colossus for ideas and initiatives that distinguished him not only in the eyes of his contemporaries but in those of history down to the present day.

Las Casas' legacy arose in large part from a potent mix of polemical single-mindedness, voluminous output, and indefatigable productivity. Yet he also survived far beyond the normal life expectancy for an active individual in the 16th century. He outlived three monarchs of Castile—Isabella I (1451–1504), Philip I (1478–1506), and Ferdinand II of Aragon (1452–1516) as well as the Emperor Charles V (1500–1558).[2] But such unusually long life was not a unique achievement for that age. Some comparisons with other luminaries of his time show a wide range of ages. Las Casas lived about as long as the eminent and long-serving Franciscan at court, Cardinal Francisco Jiménez de Cisneros (1436–1517), who died at age eighty-one; or the famous Mexican Archbishop, Juan de Zumárraga (1468–1548), who died at age eighty. The great antagonist of Las Casas, Juan Ginés de Sepúlveda (1490–1573) lived for eighty-three years. Bernal Díaz del Castillo (1492 [?]–1581), the intrepid foot soldier who accompanied Hernán Cortés to Mexico and Honduras in the 1520s and 1530s, died at an estimated eighty-nine years of age.[3] Despite these cases, normal life expectancy was shorter

---

[1] Cardinal Cisneros also conferred the title, which carried a modest stipend, on other priests beside Las Casas. See Consuelo Varela, ed., *Bartolomé de las Casas: Brevísima relación de la destruición de las Indias* (Madrid: Editorial Castalia, 1999), p. 16.

[2] Technically, Ferdinand II was regent of Castile after the death of his wife, Isabella I, and the premature death—some say by poisoning—of their son, Philip I.

[3] Francisco Jimenez de Cisneros had a long and distinguished life. A Franciscan, he was imprisoned during the period 1473–1479 by the archbishop of Toledo during the Castilian war of succession but survived to be named prelate of Sigüenza in 1482. Two

during the 16th century, even for nonwarriors who died peacefully in bed. Hernán Cortés (1485–1547), the ambitious, indefatigable conqueror of Mexico, died at age sixty-two. Antonio de Mendoza (ca. 1490–1552), the first viceroy of New Spain, also died at age sixty-two. Christopher Columbus (1451–1506), the ill-fated explorer who crossed the Atlantic almost as many times as Las Casas, died at age fifty-five. Pedro de Mendoza (1487–1537), the wealthy aristocratic conquistador who founded the distant Argentine city of Buenos Aires, died at age fifty. The famous Carmelite nun Saint Teresa of Avila (1515–1582), died at sixty-seven years, but her mother died at age thirty-three, having had twelve children. Las Casas lived at the same time as many important 16th-century characters in Spanish history and, surprisingly, met a large number of them.[4] And it seemed that he eagerly grasped every opportunity that came his way. As an active, well-connected man of his times, he helped shape history and his emerging Atlantic world. From many perspectives his story is indeed a most unusual one.

As a young, peripatetic Spanish colonist in the Americas, Las Casas manifested an insatiable passion for material wealth. Later, when he abruptly embraced the cause of social and political justice for the indigenous population of the Americas—sometime after 1514—it became his magnificent, all-consuming obsession. He pursued that single cause relentlessly for the rest of his life—in the Americas, at the Spanish court, and even to the Pope in Rome. Thus, Bartolomé de las Casas was the first full-time advocate of the underprivileged in the history of the Americas. He was also, despite a long, roving career, a tireless archivist and a prolific writer of reports, treatises, and histories. He

---

years later he joined the Franciscan order and quickly rose in importance. In 1492 he became confessor to Queen Isabella and provincial of the Franciscan order of Castile in 1494. The following year, he became archbishop of Toledo and primate of Spain. Under his primacy the Moors of Granada were forcibly converted to Catholicism or expelled from Spain, an edict that led to the great revolt of the Moors between 1499 and 1500. He became a cardinal in 1507 as well as the inquisitor general for Castile and León. He joined an expedition that captured Oran on the North African coast in 1509 and served briefly as regent of Castile in 1516 until the arrival of Charles I from the Netherlands. Juan de Zumárraga, also a member of the Franciscan order, served as the first bishop appointed to Mexico in 1527. Although sympathetic to the native peoples, he accepted the ruling of Trent that declared deviations from Rome to be heretical, and he burned a large number of Aztec manuscripts as heretical writings. He oversaw the expansion of Catholicism in Mexico and Central America and in 1547 was appointed archbishop of New Spain.

[4] The biographical data summarized in this paragraph is largely derived from *Webster's New Biographical Dictionary* (Springfield, MA: Merriam-Webster Publishers, 1983).

collected everything he could lay his hands on. He had access to copies of the journals of Columbus—his summary is the only extant copy of that illustrious document—and his living quarters were also extensive libraries. Las Casas was the perfect example of the 16th-century activist-scholar. In many ways Las Casas helped shape the jurisprudential nature of the Spanish American colonial world. His anti-imperial and anticolonial arguments continue to resonate in the contemporary world wherever the contests between rich and poor, powerful and powerless, strong and weak, atavistic and altruistic, continue to be played out.

The haunting shadow of Las Casas loomed over the important first phases of the Spanish exploration, occupation, and administration of the Americas. George Sanderlin has cogently captured the enormous impact of Las Casas on the early post-Columbian history of the Americas:

> Las Casas' life extended through the first seventy-four years of Spanish discovery and conquest of the New World. Indeed, Las Casas took a *pars magna* in the astounding events by which Spain claimed an empire stretching from Canada to the Strait of Magellan. He crossed the Atlantic ten times, sailed the Pacific, participated in the conquest of Cuba, converted warlike natives of Guatemala, attended church conferences in Mexico City, and fought for the Indians before New World *audiencias* [colonial juridical courts] and, above all, at the peripatetic Spanish court.[5]

The biographical details of the early life of Bartolomé de las Casas, like that of most ordinary people of his time, are not very well known. He was certainly born in the Triana section of Seville, the important, prosperous Andalucian city on the banks of the Guadalquivir River that meanders through the beautiful fertile plains of southern Spain.[6] Las Casas often referred to himself as a native of Seville, and on that there is strong scholarly consensus. Beyond that scholars are sharply divided as to whether he was born in August 1474 or as much as ten years later, on November 11, 1484. In that age of excessively high infant mortality, no

---

[5] George Sanderlin, ed., *Witness: Writings of Bartolomé de las Casas* (Maryknoll, NY: Orbis Books, 1992). The *audiencia* was the regional appellate court and administrative tribunal in colonial Spanish America. The monarch appointed its members. The institution originated in ancient Castile.

[6] According to Vilma Benso de Ferrer, Las Casas was born in the Triana section of Seville in 1474. See Vilma Benso de Ferrer, *Pasajeros a La Española, 1492–1530* (Santo Domingo: Benso de Ferrer, 2000), p. 81. As the next footnote indicates, most recent publications have accepted the later date of 1484 proposed by Helen R. Parish and H. E. Weidman.

national registry of births existed. The first significant event for any newborn was probably baptism around the age of one year. Birthdays had
relatively less significance for the individual than saint's days, hence the
confusion over so many actual birthdays as well as the notion that Las
Casas was born in August on the feast day of Saint Bartholomew.[7] More
important than the year of birth for our purposes, however, was the mo-
mentous profile of the age in which Las Casas grew up. He was born in
an extraordinarily fascinating and dynamic period not only of Spanish
but also of world history.[8] In Spain, the Catholic Christians, finally
united under the uneasy crowns of Castile and Aragon, after a struggle

---

[7] Scholarly opinion is sharply divided on the year of birth of Las Casas. In an age
when birthdays were seldom officially recorded, most men—even important men—did
not know their own birth year. Las Casas was never clear on his specific age in his various
writings and depositions and that contributed to the confusion. Both the *Encyclopedia of
Latin America*, ed. Helen Delpar (New York: McGraw Hill, 1974) and the *Encyclopedia
of Historians and Historical Writing*, ed. Kelley Boyd (Chicago: Dearborn Publishers,
1999) give the year of his birth as 1474. Manuel Giménez Fernández (1896–1968), one of
the foremost Lascasian scholars, insists that Las Casas was born in 1474. He begins his introductory essay in Juan Friede and Benjamin Keen, eds., *Bartolomé de las Casas in History* (DeKalb: Northern Illinois University Press, 1971), p. 67: "According to data
contained in his own works or in other reliable documents, Bartolomé de las Casas was
born in Seville in 1474, almost certainly in the month of August and perhaps on the
twenty-fourth day, to a canonical marriage between Pedro de las Casas, a native of Tarifa
and of Segovian stock, and a woman of Seville, very probably Isabel de Sosa, who belonged to a petit bourgeois family of Seville and owned a baker's shop and an oven for bak-
ing bread." The most persuasive case for a later date is Helen Rand Parish, with Harold E.
Weidman, S. J. "The Correct Birthdate of Bartolomé de las Casas," in *Hispanic American
Historical Review* 56:3 (1976): 385–403. They write: "Bartolomé de las Casas was born almost a decade later than has been believed—definitely in 1484 or 1485, and most probably on November 11, 1484." Some later accounts accept this 1484 date. These include:
D. A. Brading, *The First America: The Spanish Monarchy, Creole Patriots, and the Liberal
State 1492–1867* (Cambridge: Cambridge University Press, 1991); Anthony Pagden in his
introduction to *A Short Account of the Destruction of the Indies*, edited and translated by
Nigel Griffin (London: Penguin Books, 1992); George Sanderlin, ed., *Witness: Writings
of Bartolomé de las Casas* (Maryknoll, NY: Orbis Books, 1992); Mauricio Beuchot, *Bartolomé de las Casas (1484–1566)* (Madrid: Ediciones de Oro, 1995); and Consuelo
Varela, ed., *Bartolomé de las Casas, Brevísima Relación de la destruición de las Indias*
(Madrid: Editorial Castalia, 1999). As noted above, Vilma Benso de Ferrer accepts a birth
date of 1474. Both Sanderlin and Beuchot have chronologies of the life of Las Casas. The
earlier date seems more likely if it is true that Bartolomé de las Casas fought along with
the militias from Seville against the Moors who revolted in Granada in 1497. Notwithstanding the important family connections, his seniority might also have been a partial
factor in his remarkably rapid material success in America. On the other hand, Las Casas
may have been young and precocious.

[8] See Philip D. Curtin, *The World and the West: The European Challenge and
Overseas Response in the Age of Empire* (Cambridge: Cambridge University Press, 2000).

lasting more than 700 years at last expelled the Muslim Moors from southern Spain, especially from the Moors' splendid fortress city of Granada. At the same time Christopher Columbus and, later, Ferdinand Magellan (ca. 1480–1521), sailing under the auspices of Castile, opened up vast opportunities for continuing conquest, exploration, and spiritual service in the hemisphere of the Americas and across the Pacific Ocean.[9]

But Spain was not alone in expanding beyond the European continent. Extracontinental exploration represented a European-wide phenomenon. Just about every new European nation state was busy exploring beyond the frontiers of Europe. Pedro Alvars Cabral (ca. 1467–1520), Bartholomew Dias (ca. 1450–1500), and Vasco da Gama (1460–1524) carried Portuguese commercial interests to China and the Pacific and Indian Oceans.[10] The internationalist navigators and mapmakers John Cabot (ca. 1450–1499) and his son Sebastian Cabot (ca. 1476–1557) commissioned by the English crown, discovered Newfoundland and brought English fishermen as far south as Cape Cod. The Florentine Giovanni da Verrazano (ca. 1485–1528) and the Frenchman Jacques Cartier (1491–1557) spread early French influence from the St. Lawrence River valley in Canada to the mouth of the Hudson River in New York.[11] Exploration and conquest, often as transnational enterprises, were taking place at a breathtakingly rapid rate. Spain and Europe—as well as the rest of the world—would never be the same thereafter.[12]

Las Casas' mother, Isabel de Sosa, was probably from a conventional and well-connected Catholic family. Her cousin Juan de Sosa, was a distinguished conquistador in Peru. Isabel de Sosa died about 1497, at a

---

[9] Ferdinand Magellan—Fernão de Magalhães in Portuguese and Fernando de Magallanés in Spanish—was a Portuguese nobleman who entered Spanish service in 1517 after distinguished exploration under the auspices of the Portuguese crown. In 1519 he set out from Spain with five ships, sailed around the southern tip of South America through the straits that bear his name, and discovered the Philippines, where local inhabitants killed him. The expedition continued, and one of his ships returned to Spain in 1522.

[10] See A. J. R. Russell-Wood, *A World on the Move: The Portuguese in Africa, Asia, and America 1415–1808* (New York: St. Martin's Press, 1992). See also J. H. Parry, *The Age of Reconnaissance: Discovery, Exploration, and Settlement, 1450–1650* (London: The World Publishing Company, 1963).

[11] Patrick O'Brien, ed., *Philip's Atlas of World History from the Origins of Humanity to the Year 2000* (London: George Philip Limited, 1999), pp. 116–7.

[12] See J. H. Elliott, *Imperial Spain, 1469–1716* (New York: St. Martin's Press, 1963).

time when her husband was away in the New World and her son, Bartolomé, may have been helping to suppress a Moorish revolt in Granada.[13] Las Casas' father, Pedro de las Casas, was an energetic, upwardly-mobile, but struggling minor businessman who derived from the group of Jewish converts to Catholicism called *conversos*. He was from the small town of Tarifa near Cadiz. The family originally came from Segovia and was related to the notorious short-lived conquistador Pedrarías Dávila of Darién fame.[14] Pedro de las Casas, along with three of his brothers, Diego, Gabriel, and Francisco de Peñalosa, accompanied Christopher Columbus on his second voyage to the New World in September 1493.[15] Pedro and Isabel gave their son a good education. The voluminous writings of Bartolomé de las Casas reflect an excellent command of Latin and ancient history, indicating an early classical religious education, probably acquired in the cathedral school in Granada that was later directed by the famous philologist Elío Antonio de Nebrija (1441–1522; Nebrija was the first to construct a grammar of the Castilian language, dedicating it to Queen Isabella as the perfect instrument of empire). Las Casas' early life in Seville is not well known, but that is not surprising. As indicated above, he may have participated in the Moorish uprising in Granada in 1497, but if so, his participation lacked distinction, or he might indeed have been a minor.

The modern historian Benjamin Keen thought the Las Casas family background to be unpretentious:

> The studies of Manuel Giménez Fernández have dispelled much of the obscurity surrounding Las Casas' early life. The tradition linking him to the great noble house of Casas or Casaus has no basis in fact; his father

---

[13] Details in Friede and Keen, *Las Casas*, pp. 67–9. If Las Casas was born in 1484, it is unlikely that he would have been old enough to participate in this event. See also note 7 on p. xiv.

[14] Pedrarías Dávila, also known as Pedro Arias de Avila, was born about 1440 in Segovia and arrived in Darién in 1514 as governor of that ill-fated Spanish base of operations. His difficult, ruthless, and contested rule brought him the nickname *Furor Dominini*. Among other evils, he executed the conquistador Vasco Núñez de Balboa, the founder of Panama, on unsubstantiated charges of treason in 1519. He was later appointed governor of Nicaragua, where he died in 1530. See Mark Burkholder and Lyman Johnson, *Colonial Latin America*, 4th ed. (New York: Oxford University Press, 2001), p. 39.

[15] Friede and Keen, *Las Casas*, p. 67. It was not uncommon for brothers, especially among the aspiring nobility, to give themselves pretentious last names, so the fact that one of the brothers of Bartolomé de las Casas had a different last name is noteworthy but not unusual.

was a modest merchant, his sister married a carpenter. He did not study at or graduate from the University of Salamanca, although he studied Latin and the humanities at Seville.[16]

As an impressionable youth—he would have been between eight and eighteen—Bartolomé de las Casas witnessed the enthusiastic parades in Seville to commemorate the return of Christopher Columbus from his first voyage of discovery in 1493. On that occasion, Columbus displayed the seven brightly decorated Indians he brought back with him from the New World, along with some gorgeously colored parrots, painted native masks, several curiosities, and a small sample of gold. A rubber ball that could bounce far higher than any ball he had known before especially impressed Las Casas. The Columbus display was a highly successful recruiting technique for the second voyage, attracting as it did three male members of the Las Casas family and many of those who would later achieve great fame in the New World.[17] In sharp contrast with the immense difficulty of mounting the initial expedition, the second voyage of Columbus attracted some 1,500 eager participants, representing a veritable cross section of Spanish society at the time.[18]

[16] Benjamin Keen, *The Aztec Image in Western Thought* (New Brunswick, NJ: Rutgers University Press, 1971), pp. 92–3.

[17] Among the 1,500 travelers accompanying Columbus on his second voyage in 1493 were court physician Dr. Diego Chanca; Juan de la Cosa; Diego de Velásquez, who discovered Cuba; Francisco de Garay, the first effective governor of Jamaica; Miguel Díaz, founder of the town of Santo Domingo on Hispaniola and later San Germán in Puerto Rico; Juan Ponce de León, who explored Florida; Alonso de Ojeda; Francisco Roldán; and the three Las Casas men. See Troy S. Floyd, *The Columbus Dynasty in the Caribbean, 1492–1526* (Albuquerque: University of New Mexico Press, 1973), pp. 17–24; and David M. Traboulay, *Columbus and Las Casas: The Conquest and Christianization of America, 1492–1566* (Lanham, MD: University Press of America, 1994), p. 24. Also along with Columbus was the young Jeronymite friar Ramón Pané, who wrote the first European account of the people of Hispaniola in 1498. Pané's account influenced some early works such as that of the Italian Peter Martyr's *Decades of the New World*. Peter Martyr, of course, never traveled to the New World. See Fray Ramón Pané, *An Account of the Antiquities of the Indians*, a new edition with an introductory study, notes, and appendixes by José Juan Arrom, translated by Susan C. Griswold (Durham, NC: Duke University Press, 1999).

[18] This would be the pattern for all succeeding ventures to the Americas. See Ida Altman, *Emigrants and Society: Extremadura and America in the Sixteenth Century* (Berkeley: University of California Press, 1989); Encarnación Lemus López, *Ausente en Indias: Una historia de la emigración a America* (Madrid: Junta de Extremadura, 1993); and Rosario Márquez Macías, *La emigración española á America (1765–1824)* (Oviedo: Universidad de Oviedo, n.d.).

Thereafter the Indies became a powerful magnet for the restless populations of Spain. When Pedro de las Casas returned to Spain in 1498 or
1499, he presented his son with a young Taino Indian. Liberated by
order of Queen Isabella in 1500, the Indian returned to the Indies, but
for Bartolomé the early exposure would generate a fascination that
would last a lifetime.[19] Remarkably, within two years Las Casas, the lit-
tle-known expectant colonist, and his Indian acquaintance were reconciled in Hispaniola.

In 1502, when he was between eighteen and twenty-eight—a mature
age for his time—Bartolomé de las Casas accompanied his father in the
large initial colonizing expedition led by Nicolás de Ovando (ca.
1451–ca. 1511) designed to occupy and settle effectively the recently
discovered Caribbean island of Hispaniola.[20] After that date, the story of
Las Casas' life would become very well known, and he would seldom be
far from the limelight. Pedro de las Casas received an *encomienda*,[21] or
official allotment of Indians, and proceeded to mine for gold. His son
Bartolomé started his American sojourn working as a paid *doctrinero*, or

[19] Sanderlin, ed., *Witness*, p. 2.

[20] Las Casas would be twenty-eight if born in 1474. Ovando's expedition brought
some 1,500 settlers to Hispaniola. Sailing under the auspices of the crown, this represented a major turning point in the Spanish relationship with the Americas. Not only did
the colonizing expedition undermine the authority previously granted to Columbus,
but it also reflected the transformation of the overseas enterprise from trading to true
settlement.

[21] The *encomienda* was an ancient Spanish tradition of tribute collected by designated noble individuals and certain military orders from towns, especially towns recaptured from the Moors. In the New World it involved what Charles Gibson in *The Aztecs
Under Spanish Rule* calls, "a system of private labor and jurisdiction" (p. 26). He also
noted that

In legal principle, *encomienda* was a benign agency for Indian Hispanization. Its
essential feature was the official consignment of groups of Indians to privileged
Spanish colonists. The grantees, called *encomenderos*, were entitled to receive
tribute and labor from the Indians delegated to them. The Indians, though liable
to the demands for tribute and labor during the effective period of the grant, were
regarded as free for the reason that they were not owned as property by their *encomenderos*. Their freedom established a legal distinction between *encomienda*
and slavery, and between *encomienda* and more refined types of feudal tenure. A
grant of *encomienda* conferred no landed property, judicial jurisdiction, do-
minium, or *señorío* [lordship]. It entrusted to each *encomendero* the Christian wel-
fare of a designated number of Indians. *Encomienda* was a possession, not
property, and it was per se inalienable and non-inheritable, save insofar as the
terms of particular grants might allow. A vacant (unpossessed) *encomienda* re-
verted to the monarch, who might retain its Indians under royal administration or
reissue them to a new *encomendero*. (p. 58)

lay teacher of religious doctrine, thereby utilizing his command of Latin. Apparently it was as remunerative an occupation as any other, since within a short time Las Casas became a moderately wealthy man. From Ovando he had also received an *encomienda* for his personal service, near Concepción de La Vega in the densely populated northern region of the island. The *encomienda* represented the lucrative tribute system worked out by Queen Isabella of Castile whereby the Crown retained possession of the newly discovered lands while the arriving colonists enjoyed usufruct, along with a designated number of Indians to work the land for the Spanish.[22] In return, the Spanish colonists were obliged to instruct the Indians in the Catholic faith as well as to pay them a modest wage as repeatedly stipulated in the Laws of Burgos of 1512, and later, the so-called New Laws of 1542. Those conditions constituted an integral component of the much-debated theory of "just right," the moral justification and sort of quid pro quo permitting the Spanish to occupy the newly found lands.[23] While the officially "encommended" Indians were not legally slaves—that is, they could not be sold or transferred freely—they remained nevertheless ruthlessly exploited, as Las Casas repeated often in his various writings.[24] Las Casas helped suppress the Indian rebellion at Higuey, on the eastern part of Hispaniola—a brutal event that he described in his *Brevísima Relación de la Destruición de las Indias* (rendered in this edition by the title, *An Account, Much Abbreviated, of the Destruction of the Indies*). He later accompanied Diego de Velásquez y Cuéllar (1465–1524) to Cuba as chaplain of an expedition in 1513, having been ordained a few years before. For his services in Cuba, Las Casas received jointly with one Pedro de Rentería a second *encomienda* of Indians living along the Arimao River between Cienfuegos and Trinidad. While he apparently went into

---

See Gibson, *The Aztecs Under Spanish Rule*, p. 26 and p. 58. Also, Lesley Byrd Simpson, *The Encomienda in New Spain: The Beginnings of Spanish Mexico* (Berkeley: The University of California Press, 1966), and Robert Himmerich y Valencia, *The Encomenderos of New Spain, 1521–1555* (Austin: The University of Texas Press, 1991).

[22] The best monograph on the *encomienda* remains, Simpson, *The Encomienda in New Spain*. For the history of the *encomienda* in Hispaniola see Floyd, *The Columbus Dynasty*, and Altman, *Emigrants and Society*, pp. 221–5. Individuals and corporate entities like the church and towns were, at the pleasure of the Crown, given lands in outright grants called *mercedes*.

[23] Lewis Hanke, *The Spanish Struggle for Justice in the Conquest of America* [originally published by the AHA in Washington DC, 1949] (Boston: Little, Brown, 1965), pp. 17–36.

[24] Indians who resisted Spanish efforts to subordinate them were enslaved, as were those who fought against the Spanish.

large-scale international commerce, there is no evidence that he paid much attention to his obligation to attend to the spiritual well-being of his Indian charges. The Las Casas-Rentería cattle and agricultural enterprises prospered enough for them to be a major supplier of foodstuff, cattle, and slaves to Jamaica, Puerto Rico, Santo Domingo, and even as far away as Darién on the Isthmian mainland.[25] Although Las Casas abandoned his economic pursuits and surrendered his *repartimiento*, or official allocation, of Indians in 1514, he had already amassed enough wealth to support himself for several years traveling back and forth across the Atlantic and living at court in Spain.[26]

In the combined capacity of warrior, priest, and merchant, Las Casas traveled extensively throughout the Caribbean and Isthmian mainland during his first twelve years in the region. He witnessed many of the callously brutal initial encounters between Spaniards and Indians on several islands as well as various locations on the mainland. This personal eye-witnessing would be the basis for his "true account" later, when he renounced the pursuit of riches to become the indefatigable advocate of civil and human rights for the indigenous peoples of the Americas. His credibility depended largely on his personal identification with the people and events of which he spoke. This Las Casas repeats frequently, as when he speaks about the situation in Cuba:

> In the three or four months that I abode there, above seven thousand children starved to death, because their fathers and mothers had been carried off to the mines. *And many other such heinous things of that kind did I see.* [Emphasis added]

Las Casas became an ordained priest in 1510 and eventually joined the Dominican order in 1522. He had been slowly reevaluating his Caribbean experience and had occasionally protested the extremely harsh treatment of some Indians at the hands of Spanish *conquistadores.* But Las Casas was not the first to protest the ill treatment of the Indians publicly. That distinction belonged to the Dominican priest Antonio de Montesinos (d. ca. 1545), who preached two powerfully disturbing sermons in late November and early December of 1511 in Santo Domingo.[27] A graduate of the University of Salamanca, Montesinos ar-

---

[25] Friede and Keen, *Las Casas*, p. 73.

[26] A *repartimiento* was a legal distribution of tributary Indians and was often the synonym for *encomienda* throughout Spanish America.

[27] Biographical details on Father Antonio de Montesinos are extremely scarce. He arrived in Hispaniola in 1510 and preached his famous sermon in 1511. He is supposed to have been martyred in the Americas. See Felix Jay, *Three Dominican Pioneers in the New*

rived in Hispaniola with the first cohort of missionaries in 1510, about the same time that Las Casas was ordained. The texts of his sermons had the unqualified support of his superior as well as his fraternal peers, who defended him against the vicious attacks of the colonists. Later he would be sent to Spain to defend the order, his sermons, and himself before King Ferdinand. Even though Montesinos went armed with "a file containing a document divided into chapters and listing the atrocities in war and peace inflicted on the Indians of the island, all well authenticated and all perpetrated by Spanish colonists,"[28] securing an audience with the monarch proved a long, arduous, and discouraging task. Nevertheless, Montesinos succeeded.

Montesinos reproached his fellow Spaniards and threatened them with dire consequences for their gross mistreatment of the local inhabitants. His first sermon stated:

> In order to make your sins known to you I have mounted this pulpit, I who am the voice of Christ crying in the wilderness of this island; and therefore it behooves you to listen to me, not with indifference but with all your heart and senses; for this voice will be the strangest, the harshest, the most terrifying that you have ever heard or expected to hear. . . . Tell me, by what right or justice do you hold these Indians in such cruel and horrible slavery? By what right do you wage such detestable wars on these people who lived mildly and peacefully in their own lands, where you have consumed infinite numbers of them with unheard of murders and desolations? . . . Are they not men? Do they not have rational souls? Are you not bound to love them as you love yourselves? How can you live in such profound and lethargic slumber? Be sure that in your present state you can no more be saved than the Moors or Turks who do not have and do not want the faith of Jesus Christ.[29]

Although he did not personally hear the sermons, Las Casas could not have missed hearing the tremendous negative uproar among the Spanish settlers who took the matter of the meddling priest to the council of the monarch in Castile. Montesinos advocated nothing short of a termination of the systems of *encomienda* and *repartimiento* of Indians, whose consequence would be the creation of an egalitarian society in

---

World: *Antonio de Montesinos, Domingo de Betanzos, Gonzalo Lucero* (Lewiston, NY: Edwin Mellen Press, 2002), pp. 3–4 and 18–32.

[28] The quotation is taken from Jay, *Three Dominican Pioneers*, p. 29.

[29] Benjamin Keen, ed., *Readings in Latin-American Civilization: 1492 to the Present*, 2d ed. (Boston: Houghton Mifflin Company, 1955), p. 88. This is a translation of the account given by Las Casas in his *Historia de las Indias*, chapters 4–6. A slightly different and less graceful translation may be found in Jay, *Three Dominican Pioneers*, pp. 18–9.

which everyone worked on his own behalf and recently arriving Spanish immigrants would be placed on the same footing as the indigenous inhabitants. Such a situation would have severely undermined the rapacious ambitions of the Spanish colonists, whose desire for wealth was not predicated on actually working for it themselves. Nor was Montesinos alone in protesting the deplorable conditions of early Spanish colonization in the Americas. Other early Dominican and Franciscan priests, both on the islands and the mainland, also spoke out against the brutality of the conquest and the system of arbitrarily enslaving Indians.

No one, however, would pursue his protest as far as Bartolomé de las Casas. After the sermons of Montesinos, Las Casas slowly underwent a spiritual epiphany. His restlessness was undoubtedly fueled by the extensive agitation among the colonists as well as his increasing spiritual turmoil over being a slave owner, especially in Cuba. Indeed, his moment of truth came in Baracoa, a remote settlement in northeastern Cuba, in 1514, as he was preparing a Sunday sermon for his small flock and meditating on some relevant spiritual texts. Suddenly his future mission came to him, as Las Casas himself admitted, as he reflected on some verses from the book of Ecclesiasticus.[30]

> That began, I tell you, a consideration of the misery and suffering of those wretched people [the Indians]. I reflected on what I had heard spoken about of what was going on in Española and how the priests in Santo

---

[30] The personal reference may be found in Bartolomé de las Casas, *Historia de las Indias*, Book III, chapter 79. I have used the three-volume edition edited by André Saint-Lu (Caracas: Biblioteca Ayacucho, 1986), in which the Latin text of the impressive verses is quoted by Las Casas. Las Casas would have been using, of course, a Latin version of the Catholic Bible, the Vulgate that contained Ecclesiasticus, one of the "apocryphal" prophets. The text that moved Las Casas should not be confused with the book of Ecclesiastes in the familiar King James Version of the Bible. The King James Version of the English Bible, translated in 1611 after Las Casas' time, has only twelve chapters in Ecclesiastes—all of them equally quotable and moving—but no book of Ecclesiasticus, nor many other books found in the Latin Vulgate. In personal communications both from Fr. Stafford Poole and from Andrew Hurley, for which I am enormously grateful, they point out that Ecclesiasticus, also called Sirach, is the longest book in the Catholic Bible, more than fifty chapters. According to Hurley, Las Casas was especially impressed with chapter 34 "and the relevant quotation from verses 21 and 22, though 22 is supposed to be the key. . . . *He slays his neighbor who deprives him of his living; he sheds blood who denies the laborer his wages.*" [Emphasis added.] Fr. Poole suggests verse 18 (although Las Casas himself says that he was especially impressed by verse [perhaps chapter ?] 34). The event can also be followed in Henry Raup Wagner with the collaboration of Helen Rand Parish, *The Life and Writings of Bartolomé de las Casas* (Albuquerque: The University of New Mexico Press, 1967), pp. 11–3. The Wagner-Parish account takes some liberties with the original text.

Domingo used to say that no one with a clear conscience could enslave Indians, and that furthermore they would refuse to offer confession or absolution to anyone who had slaves, something one well-known clergyman did not accept. This same clergyman found himself once with another cleric of that order [the Dominicans] and although having some slaves in Española and demonstrating the same indifference and blindness shown in the island of Cuba, he wanted to make a confession. But the cleric would not accept his confession.[31]

In 1515, on the pretext that he needed to study in France, Las Casas secured permission to leave his parish of Sancti Spíritus in Cuba and travel to Spain, via Santo Domingo, to plead his newly discovered cause of justice for the Indians of the Americas, which he never after abandoned. By December of that year Las Casas found himself at court, pleading his case to a king who would die within the month. The following year he had better luck with the aging but still important Cardinal Francisco Jiménez de Cisneros, and he was rewarded with the title of "Protector of the Indians."[32] He submitted three treatises that were influential in the appointment of a reform commission entrusted to the Jeronymites, presumably as a neutral force between the ubiquitous, energetic Dominicans and humble, curious, millennial Franciscans who accompanied the early settlers to the Americas. But Spanish court politics was extremely complex and factionalized, and influencing court action was not an easy matter. Las Casas adroitly managed to get the ear of the young Emperor, Charles V, who granted him about 200 leagues of the Venezuelan coast on which to implement a novel project: a free community of productive Indians loyal to the monarchs of Castile — and creating it without war and bloodshed.[33] While it was far less than his original ambitious request of one thousand leagues of coastline, Las Casas was not dismayed. Leaving Spain in 1520 with a small number of eccentric recruits at the height of the *Comunero* revolts, Las Casas sailed for the site of his proposed colony.[34] The colony of peaceful farmers was

---

[31]Las Casas, *Historia de las Indias*, ed. Saint-Lu, Vol. III, p. 283. The translation is done by the author. In the 16th century the Spanish referred to Hispaniola as Española. Note that Las Casas is relating a personal experience that many writers subsequently consider to be the turning point in his attitude toward the Spanish colonization of the Americas.

[32] Charles V also gave this title to then-bishop Juan de Zumárraga for his work in defense of the Indians of New Spain in 1527 and to bishop-designate of Guatemala, Francisco Marroquín, in 1532.

[33] Details may be followed in Brading, *The First America*, pp. 58–101.

[34] The Comunero revolts were a series of urban riots in 1520 and 1521 throughout cities in Castile that seriously threatened the reign of the new young monarch, Charles V.

to be based near Cumaná — unfortunately close to the pearl fisheries at Cubagua and their insatiable need for slaves. By the time Las Casas reached Puerto Rico, news from the mainland was bad, and it got even worse by the time he arrived in Santo Domingo.[35] The Indians along the Venezuelan coast had completely destroyed two earlier mission villages, and the Spanish colonists on the island were yearning not only for revenge but also for more indigenous slaves. Listening to sermons that exhorted them to be peaceful was not an attractive proposition to people who were capturing Indians for slaves, or to Indians who found that employing force against the Spaniards was indispensable for their personal security. Moreover, farming was not an attractive proposition for those who signed up for the expedition. Spaniards coming to the Indies spurned manual labor unless it was in hand-to-hand combat. They all wanted to get rich by exploiting Indians or finding gold. The attempt to establish a new mission quickly ended in utter fiasco, with most of the founding party of Spanish settlers deserting their spiritual leader. In early 1522, discouraged by this experience, Las Casas entered the Dominican monastery in Santo Domingo to reflect on his failed mission. Some time later he took his vows and was named prior to the small town of Puerto Plata on the north shore of the island of Hispaniola.[36]

When Las Casas arrived in Puerto Plata in May 1526, the town had about thirty *encomenderos*, indicating a significant number of available Indians.[37] As the name of the town implies, the Spanish had begun the local production of silver, and they supplemented their metal exports by killing and skinning the wild cattle that had multiplied prodigiously on the island. Within a year, Las Casas built a substantial church of stone and mud and started to write his monumental *Historia de las Indias* [History of the Indies], recounting in meticulous detail the extensive Caribbean and circum-Caribbean empire established by Spain in the first decades of the 16th century. Las Casas also gathered a great amount of material on Hispaniola, Jamaica, Cuba, Puerto Rico, and Terra Firma (the continental lands of Central and South America) that would serve as the basis for his later writings in Spain. By 1531 a restless Las Casas had resumed his advocacy of Indian rights. He wrote a long

[35] Hanke, *The Spanish Struggle*, pp. 66–71.

[36] Friede and Keen, *Las Casas*, pp. 84–5.

[37] *Encomenderos* derived their wealth and sustenance from the tribute and service provided by the Indians held in *encomienda*. Since assignment was usually by Indian heads of households, it is reasonable to assume that several hundred families of Indians must have lived in the environs of Puerto Plata.

letter to the Council of the Indies describing the demographic devastation wrought by the Spanish settlers in the New World and warning that such activity could have calamitous consequences not only for Spain but also, and especially, for its esteemed monarch. In particular, he pointed out that violence patently violated the spirit of the Alexandrine Bulls,[38] which conferred the territory to Castile, as well as the royal testament of Queen Isabella who saw herself as carrying out the Divine Will in spreading the "True Faith" to those unknown lands.[39] In making that argument Las Casas affirmed that violence could only be justified in cases of prior occupancy of the land or if the inhabitants were infidels—both of which were highly dubious in the case of the Americas. Between 1531 and 1533 Las Casas traveled to Mexico, where he renewed his friendship with Hernán Cortés as well as with the upwardly mobile Franciscan friar Juan de Zumárraga in Mexico City and with the Dominican Julian Garcés (1457–1547) in Tlaxcala. Las Casas also made a journey to Puerto Rico. But his opposition to the enslavement of the Indians and his vociferous advocacy of Indians rights attracted an increasing number of powerful political enemies. As a result, his superiors recalled him to Santo Domingo.

Santo Domingo in the 1530s was the most important Spanish city in the Americas. Apart from being the cradle of the broader Spanish American colonizing enterprise, the town witnessed the temporary sojourn of almost all the significant people who made history at that time. It was a

---

[38] The Alexandrine Bulls were a series of edicts issued in 1493 by Pope Alexander VI—a Spaniard—at the request of Queen Isabella of Castile; they divided the recently discovered world between Portugal and Spain. The edicts stipulated that Spain had a monopoly over all lands discovered beyond a line arbitrarily drawn one hundred leagues west of the Cape Verde Islands. Papal edicts of this sort were commonplace at the time. In 1454 Pope Nicholas V had issued a bull awarding the Canary Islands to Portugal, along with an effective trade monopoly of all lands south of the islands. Normally these bulls implied a quid pro quo—the discover-conquerors built and maintained churches and helped support the clergy and their missionary efforts. Papal edicts at the time had considerable moral force in international relations. Nevertheless, it is interesting that despite the bulls, both Castilian and Portuguese monarchs worked out a bilateral secular accord at Tordesillas in 1494 ratifying the papal position but moving the line by mutual agreement to a position 370 leagues west of the Cape Verde Islands.

[39] Hanke, *The Spanish Struggle*. The preoccupation with justice and theology may also be followed in John Leddy Phelan, *The Millennial Kingdom of the Franciscans in the New World*, 2d ed., rev. (Berkeley: The University of California Press, 1970). Throughout the 16th century, a sharp division developed between the Dominicans—of whom Bartolomé de las Casas was one—and the Franciscans, exemplified in the writings of Gerónimo de Mendieta (1525–1604). Dominicans believed in peaceful conquest. Franciscans supported the use of force, if necessary.

superb location for Las Casas to serve his confinement after his removal
from Puerto Plata. Santo Domingo was the great crossroads where those
who had made it and those who wanted to make it congregated. Las
Casas took advantage of the opportunity to consult the archives of
Diego Columbus (1479–1526) then in the governor's palace in the city,
as well as to talk with Hernando Pizarro (ca. 1475–1578), Juan de Sosa,
and other prominent participants about the extraordinary military conquests then taking place in Peru and elsewhere on the mainland.[40] In
1535 Las Casas accompanied Fray Tomás de Berlanga (d. 1551), the
newly appointed bishop of Panama, to that city.[41] He took a trip to
Nicaragua and denounced the pacification then under way by Rodrigo
de Contreras. He also wrote a long letter to the Crown denouncing the
conquest of Peru and the military activities going on in Nicaragua. Apparently he had some beneficial result, for in July 1536 the king issued
a *cédula* (or royal decree) suspending the conquest of Nicaragua for two
years.[42] The Spanish colonists did not appreciate the intervention of Las
Casas on behalf of the Indians. Virtually expelled from Nicaragua, Las
Casas continued on to Guatemala and Mexico.

---

[40] According to Ida Altman, Hernando Pizarro followed his famous half-brother,
Francisco, to the Indies in 1530. His brothers Juan and Gonzalo also accompanied him.
Francisco first came to the Indies in 1502 in the initial expedition of Ovando. See Altman,
Emigrants and Society, pp. 9–10; also see Benso de Ferrer, *Pasajeros a la Española*, pp.
316 and 394. James Lockhart provides extensive information on all the Pizarros in his *The
Men of Cajamarca: A Social and Biographical Study of the First Conquerors of Peru*
(Austin: University of Texas Press, 1972). "Something of the nature of the Pizarro family's
dominance in the conquering expedition can be seen in the fact that Francisco was by far
the most senior figure in the Indies, while Hernando had incomparably the best position
in Spain. . . . Hernando was not only an eldest (and only) legitimate son, he had already
inherited his father's estate and was the functioning head of his family. Though the
Pizarros did not yet have a legally instituted entail, Hernando had received as inalienable
property the core of the rather meager Pizarro holdings, consisting of their family residence on the square in Trujillo and their rights to the village of La Zarza, and so in effect
he was in the envied position of a *mayorazgo*" (Lockhart, *The Men of Cajamarca*, p. 157).
Biographical details on Juan de Sosa are scarce. He arrived in Hispaniola with Diego
Columbus in 1509. Like Las Casas he served as a secular priest in his early days. He accompanied Pizarro to Peru and although he received a share of the gold and was on the
list, was not actually present at Cajamarca. See Lockhart, *The Men of Cajamarca*, pp.
465–8.

[41] Berlanga, from the town of the same name in Soria, came to Santo Domingo
about 1516. He had been a professor at the University of Salamanca. He served in various
positions in Hispaniola, Mexico, and Peru. He was bishop of Panama between 1531 and
1545. He died in the early 1550s. See Benso de Ferrer, *Pasajeros a la Española*, p. 50.

[42] Friede and Keen, *Las Casas*, p. 88.

In a long petition cosponsored by bishops Juan de Zumárraga and Julián Garcés, Las Casas wrote to Pope Paul III regarding the protection of the Indians of New Spain. The petition, written in Latin and titled "The Only Method of Attracting All People to the True Faith," advocated nothing short of a radical alteration of the method of conquest and conversion in the New World. The three clergymen essentially supported a clear separation between Spaniards and Indians in the New World, with the establishment of theocratic communities of Indians across the Americas. With support from the Spanish court and the head of the Dominican order, the petition influenced the pope to issue the celebrated papal bull *Sublimis Deus* in June 1537.[43] In its entirety the bull declared:

> Paul, bishop, servant of the servants of God, to all of Christ's faithful who will see this letter, greetings and apostolic blessings.
>
> God on high so loved the human race that he formed man in such a way that not only could he share what is good like any other creature but he could also attain the supreme, inaccessible, and invisible good and see it face-to-face. And since, by the testimony of Sacred Scripture, man was also created to reach eternal life and happiness and since no one can attain this eternal life and happiness except through the faith of Our Lord Jesus Christ, it is necessary to profess that man is of such a condition and nature that he can receive the faith of Christ and that whoever has shared human nature is capable of receiving it. Neither is anyone considered so foolish as to believe himself capable of achieving the end without in any way being concerned about the absolutely necessary means.
>
> For this reason Truth itself, which can neither deceive nor be deceived, when selecting the preachers of the faith for the office of preaching, is known to have said, "Go, teach all peoples." He said "all" without any distinction, since all are capable of instruction in the faith. Seeing and envying this, the enemy of the human race, who ever opposes all good things in order that they might perish, has devised a hitherto unheard of means for preventing the word of God from being preached to peoples for their salvation. And he has incited many of his lackeys who, desiring to fill the measure of their greed, dare to assert indiscriminately that the Indians of the west and south (and all other peoples who have come to our knowledge in these times), *on the pretext that they have no share in the Catholic faith, are to be reduced to our service like brute animals, and they enslave them, burdening them with so many afflictions such as they scarcely* [Italicized in the original] impose on the brute animals that serve them.

---

[43] Peter Bakewell, *A History of Latin America* (Oxford: Blackwell Publishers, 1997), p. 143; Parry, *The Age of Reconnaissance*, p. 311.

We, therefore, who though unworthy are the vicar of our same Lord on earth and seek with all our efforts to bring to this sheepfold the sheep of his flock entrusted to us who are still outside his sheepfold, attentive to the fact that the Indians themselves, as true men, are not only capable of the Christian faith but (as been made known to us) hasten very readily to this very faith, and wishing to provide appropriate remedies, by apostolic authority through the present letter we decree and declare that the said Indians and all other peoples who in the future will come to the knowledge of Christians, even if they are outside the Christian faith, are not deprived nor are they to be deprived of their freedom and the mastery of their possessions; rather they are able freely and lawfully to use, possess, and enjoy, freedom and ownership of this kind, nor are they to be enslaved; and whatever is done contrary to this is null and void and of no force or weight; and the Indians themselves and other peoples are to be drawn to the said faith of Christ by the preaching of the word of God and the example of the good life; and copies of the present letter written in the hand of the notary public and signed with the seal of any person in an ecclesiastical dignity are to be given the same adherence as would be given to the originals.

Anything whatever to the contrary notwithstanding.

Given at Rome at Saint Peter's, in the year of our Lord's incarnation one thousand five hundred and thirty seven, the fourth day before the nones [*nonas*] of June [June 2], in the third year of our pontificate.[44]

The essence of the bull was the unmistakable declaration that all the Indians of the Americas were rational people and therefore could not be arbitrarily enslaved by the newly arriving European colonists. It was recognition of the inherent sovereignty of the Indians of the New World. But it also implied that the American Indians were not fully capable of their own political and religious "improvement." It therefore opened the way for their mass conversion to the Catholic faith. *Sublimis Deus* was a clear victory for the ideas of Las Casas and his supporters, who had strenuously advocated recognition of Indian communal autonomy. It was less clearly so for the Castilian Crown, since it complicated the effectiveness of local administration by banning the practice of indiscriminate slavery of the Indians. It also reduced the occasions for just wars, an important economic activity of the Spanish warrior class. So-called just wars resulted after a lamentable unilateral declaration by some Spanish clergymen or any designated official like Gonzalo Fernández de Oviedo, speaking in Latin—not necessarily heard or under-

---

[44] I remain extremely grateful for this translation from the original Latin by Fr. Stafford Poole, used with his permission.

stood by the local people—that the Indians were neither spontaneously receptive to overtures of trade nor to voluntary conversion to Christianity. These wars provided a vaguely legitimate excuse for raiding Indian communities and selling the captives into slavery. Yet it was becoming increasingly evident that if the Americas were to be integrated into the Spanish political sphere, it would need large numbers of slaves to perform the principal economy-building tasks.[45] The optimal source for slaves prior to the development of the transatlantic slave trade was prisoners of war. At the time of the promulgation of the papal bull in 1537 Las Casas was in Guatemala helping to pacify that part of the Spanish colonial frontier. He returned to Mexico, where he objected to the mass baptisms of Indians—the prelate Toribio Benavente de Motolinía (ca. 1496–1569) reportedly baptized 14,000 in two days—being done especially by the Franciscans. By 1540 he returned to Spain with letters of support from a number of leading religious leaders and bureaucrats in Mexico and Guatemala.

As usual, Las Casas gave other reasons for making the trip to Spain—in this case, to recruit clergy for Guatemala and Nicaragua. He spent two years composing the *Brevísima Relación*, which was a summary of his much longer *Historia de las Indias*, suitable for presentation to the king, the Emperor Charles V. Although no names were mentioned, the vitriolic description of Spanish conduct in the New World was profusely illustrated. Describing the Indians in idyllic terms, Las Casas declared that unrestrained Spanish cruelty had virtually eliminated more than fifteen million American Indians in less than fifty years. Presumably horrified, in 1542 Charles V hurriedly issued the New Laws, designed to pacify the civil wars among Spanish colonists in Peru and bring order to all the Emperor's American possessions.[46] Neither goal was immediately achieved. The Mexican viceroy, Antonio de Mendoza,

---

[45] Despite the uncontested sincerity of the papal edict, it should be pointed out that by 1537 Spain had discovered so much precious metal in the Americas that retreat was entirely out of the question. Moreover, spreading the gospel— the injunction of the papal bull—required material resources. Production of the metals and building the infrastructure to promote evangelical work required a constantly large supply of manual labor, and the most immediate source was the neighboring Indian communities.

[46] In 1893 a nice bilingual edition of the New Laws appeared. *The New Laws of the Indies for the Good Treatment and Preservation of the Indians Promulgated by the Emperor Charles the Fifth, 1542–1543: A Facsimile Reprint of the Original Spanish Edition Together with a Literal Translation in the English Language to Which Is Prefixed an Historical Introduction By the late Henry Stevens of Vermont and Fred W. Lucas* (London: Privately printed, 1893). Stevens was described as a "sometimes student at Yale College in America."

refused to read the Laws, fearing a violent reaction on the part of the Spanish colonists.[47] The Peruvian viceroy, Blasco Núñez de Vela (d. 1546), read them with fatal consequences: The ongoing civil wars derived even greater impetus in Peru, and the viceroy lost his authority and his life.

In 1544 Emperor Charles V named Las Casas bishop of Chiapas in southern Mexico, a poor area that he preferred, instead of some important post such as Cuzco, and Las Casas set out to implement the spirit as well as the letter of the New Laws.[48] It was about this time that Las Casas asked for special permission to import African slaves, a measure he would later regret:

> That because the said bishop-elect has the intention greatly to serve God and Your Majesty by providing a means so that the lands of all the said bishopric of Chiapas and Yucatan may be settled by Spaniards, new settlers whom he plans and hopes to place therein; and also to maintain the friars who now are to travel with him to go to those said provinces, for the which he deems it necessary to sow and till farms of cassava, which are called small plantations—[therefore] he begs Your Majesty to grant him the favor of giving a license so that he may take thither two dozen Negro slaves, exempt from all duties both in Seville and in the Indies, under the condition that if he does not occupy them in the aforesaid and for the maintenance of the friars and settlers, he pay the duties to Your Majesty five-fold.[49]

It is important to recognize that in many ways Las Casas reflected the dominant mode of intellectual thought of his age. He was neither a pacifist nor an anti-imperialist nor an antislavery advocate. He believed in wars, provided they were just wars. And he believed in slavery, provided the slaves were legally acquired and treated well. In his earlier writings his advocacy of African slavery was based on the belief that Africans represented more effective workers in the tropics. That was a general European view that prevailed until well into the 19th century.

---

[47] According to David Brading, "The uproar which greeted the New Laws revealed their radical nature. In New Spain the viceroy Antonio de Mendoza invoked the power inherent in his office to suspend their implementation until the Crown had listened to the protests of the encomenderos' agents dispatched from Mexico to Spain. He also compiled a series of reports from leading institutions, including the provincials of the three mendicant orders, all of which urged caution." See Brading, *The First America*, p. 68.

[48] See Helen Rand Parrish, *Las Casas as a Bishop: A New Interpretation Based on His Holograph Petition in the Hans P. Kraus Collection of Hispanic American Manuscripts* (Washington, DC: Library of Congress, 1980), p. xi.

[49] Parrish, *Las Casas*, p. xvii.

Later Las Casas would repudiate his support for the forced enslavement of Africans.[50]

Las Casas entered his bishopric the following year inauspiciously. On March 20, 1545, he issued an order obliging all male adult heads of households (*vecinos*) to report to him within nine days on pain of excommunication. . .

> [if] there were sorcerers in the diocese, if sacrileges were committed, if there were violations of ecclesiastical immunity, if there were any cases of blasphemy, concubinage, and the like; . . . if "provisions were sold notably dearer than the price at which they should sell"; if flour was "an improper mixture"; if wine was watered and sold "as if it were good wine"; . . . if Indians were threatened with reprisals for reporting abuses, if wives and children were taken away, if their land was unjustly occupied or sold for less than its value, if their property was taken against their will, . . . if they were forced to carry excessive loads, if they were not paid for their labor, or if violence or other abuses were committed against them.[51]

What exactly Las Casas had in mind remains unclear, but the announcement was definitely not prudent. The new colonists in the Americas did not receive kindly such detailed and intrusive questionnaires, even from a bishop. Some threatened him with death, and within a short time Las Casas was on his way to Spain again. He never returned to the Americas. In 1550 he resigned his bishopric.

His adamant pro-Indian advocacy continued, however. In 1550 Las Casas conducted the famous "debate" with Juan Ginés de Sepúlveda (ca. 1490–1572?) in Valladolid, defending the native inhabitants of the Americas against the latter's charges of barbarism and natural servitude.[52] Sepúlveda, influenced by the outstanding lawyer Juan López de

---

[50] Las Casas, *Historia*, Book III, chapters 102 and 129. A discussion of Las Casas' views on slavery may be followed in Friede and Keen, *Las Casas*, pp. 165–6, and Hanke, *The Spanish Struggle*, p. 60.

[51] Friede and Keen, *Las Casas*, pp. 187–8.

[52] Las Casas and Sepúlveda never actually confronted each other during the year but kept replying in writing and in person before academics, courtiers, lawyers, and clergymen at Valladolid. Sepúlveda was a distinguished humanist of his time. Educated at Bologna and Rome, he had translated several works of Aristotle into Latin. In 1536 he was appointed imperial chronicler and later he became tutor to the future King Philip II. Las Casas made snide remarks in his works about his lack of experience in the Americas, but he had actually read many of the reports from the Americas and spoken at court with conquistadors such as Hernán Cortés and Gonzalo Fernández de Oviedo.

Valladolid is an ancient Castilian city, capital of the province of Leon in northern Spain. Recaptured from the Moors during the 10th century, it played an important role in Spanish history and was the seat of Castilian monarchs until the middle of the 16th century. Isabella married Ferdinand of Aragon there in 1469, and Philip II was born there in

Palacios Rubios (ca. 1450–1525), and the eminent Dominican clergyman Francisco de Vitoria (ca. 1486–1546), had written a treatise, *The
Second Democrates, or reasons that justify war against the Indians*, supporting the Spanish conquest of the Americas and insisting that the Indians were natural slaves.[53] The historian Anthony Pagden calls
Sepúlveda's treatise "the most virulent and uncompromising argument
for the inferiority of the American Indian ever written."[54] Sepúlveda's
argument achieved two important goals: in the first place, it established
a conveniently persuasive premise based on the innate rightness of
power that would constitute an automatically useful rationale down
through the ages for all would-be conquerors. The Indians of the Americas are, he wrote in a passage that illustrates both his classical erudition
and the strong influence of Aristotle's politics,

> barbarous, uncivilized, and inhuman people who are natural slaves, re-
> fusing to admit the superiority of those who are more prudent, powerful,
> and perfect than themselves. Their subordination would bring them
> tremendous benefits and would, besides, be a good thing by natural right
> as matter conforms to a mold, as the body to the soul, the appetite to rea-
> son, brutes to gentlemen, the wife to the husband, children to parents,
> the imperfect to the perfect, the worse to the better, all for the universal
> betterment of the whole. This is the natural order for which divine and
> eternal law requires unqualified acceptance.[55]

In the second place, it began to clarify the distinction between ethnocentricity—a preference for the familiarity of one's own people and customs—and racism—an articulated ideology of power based on notions

---

1527. Columbus died in Valladolid in 1506. Cervantes spent his last years there, writing
part of his celebrated work, *Don Quijote*. Apart from its magnificent cathedral, Valladolid
boasts a number of other landmarks, including the university, founded in 1346, and several architecturally imposing *colegios* and churches.

   [53] Hanke, *The Spanish Struggle*, pp. 113–5.

   [54] Anthony Pagden, *The Fall of Natural Man: The American Indian and the Origins of Comparative Ethnology* (Cambridge: Cambridge University Press, 1982), p. 109.

   [55] Juan Ginés de Sepúlveda, *Demócrates Segundo*. The quotation is a translation
by the author from the edited Spanish edition: Juan Ginés de Sepúlveda, *Tratado sobre las
justas causas de la guerra contra los Indios* [Treatise on just causes for war against the In-
dians], ed. Marcelino Menéndez y Pelayo and Manuel García-Pelayo (Mexico: Fondo de
Cultura Económica, 1941), p. 153. On Sepúlveda, see Angel Losada, *Juan Ginés de
Sepúlveda a través de su "epistolario" y nuevos documentos* (Madrid: Consejo Superior de
Investigaciones Científicas, 1973); Hanke, *The Spanish Struggle*; and *Actas del Congreso
Internacional V Centenario del Nacimiento del Dr. Juan Ginés de Sepúlveda celebrado en
Pozoblanco, el 13 al 16 de febrero de 1991* (Córdoba: Ayuntamiento de Pozoblanco, 1993).

of inherited characteristics found among groups categorized by race. For centuries afterwards lazy chauvinists would resort to the arguments first put forward by Sepúlveda in 1550 to justify the assumed superiority of Spaniards over non-Spaniards and one "race" over another. Sepúlveda failed to secure permission to publish *The Second Democrates*, but it was widely read and became enormously influential among some advisers at the royal court. Its publication was delayed largely as a result of the vigorous opposition mounted by Las Casas but also partly from its manifestly unsound theological assumptions.

At the time of the contest with Sepúlveda, Las Casas was living in Valladolid in a small cell in the Dominican monastery of San Gregorio. His arguments opposing Sepúlveda were outlined in a rapidly composed book published in 1553 called *Apologética historia sumaria* [A Brief Apologetic History], a lengthy discussion of Native American life and culture.[56] Not only did Las Casas refute the Aristotelian argument for natural superiority and natural inferiority—or that might was inherently right—but he also tried to show that the indigenous peoples of the Americas were in some respects more noble than the Spaniards and were only corrupted by the horrible examples of the European invaders. Logically it was not an argument that was intrinsically superior to the one presented by Sepúlveda, but Las Casas added the warning that failure to heed his words would bring unbearable afflictions on Spain and the Castilian monarchy. In this, Las Casas was supported by other churchmen, a fact that made royal officials hesitate to accept the crass advice of Juan Ginés de Sepúlveda that they could act freely in the Americas, although they were not entirely persuaded by the arguments of Las Casas, either. Moreover, by 1550 it was clear that the economic exploitation of the Americas required a large sedentary and servile population in order to continue to produce the bullion that was fast becoming a required financial diet for the new Catholic kingdom of Castile. The sense of justice and recognition of indigenous civil and human rights was tempered by pragmatism. Later Las Casas moved to Madrid and continued to write energetically—and increasingly more radically and uninhibitedly—on behalf of the American Indians, until his death on July 18, 1566.[57] By that time, the crown had begun to assert firmer control over its American possessions. The spirit of the new laws permeated the *ordenanzas* (ordinances) on discoveries and settlements pub-

---

[56] Brading, *The First Americans*, pp. 88–97.
[57] Friede and Keen, *Las Casas*, pp. 197–8.

lished in 1573, and Indians everywhere enjoyed some measure of ju-
ridical recognition.

Spain in the Age of Bartolomé de las Casas

Spain did not set out in 1492 to construct a great landed empire in the
Americas. The agreement between the Castilian monarch and Christopher Columbus indicated that both envisioned setting up commercial
relations with the Chinese along the lines then currently practiced by
the Portuguese along the African coast.[58] That would have created a
maritime trading empire with forts and factories in small enclaves in
distant lands. But instead of finding China, Columbus stumbled upon a
vast continent unknown to the Europeans. The initial generous grant
made to Columbus required substantial revision when he returned in
1493 to admit that the prospects of trade were dim but the prospects for
settlement far more promising. The fears of a rival empire—in the sense
of jurisdiction—of Spaniards overseas meant that the crown had to assume immediate control of the operation or potentially face the sort of
trouble it was encountering in Castile from the cities as well as the nobility. There was already enough trouble from the various power bases
at home to contemplate more from new ones created overseas by up-
start discoverers. The new lands had to be organized as secure royal estates. Columbus had to be quickly reduced in administrative power and
political influence.

The Spain of Ferdinand and Isabella, Christopher Columbus,
Nicolás de Ovando, Hernán Cortés, Bartolomé de las Casas, and the
other well-known figures was a dynamic and intellectually vibrant society. Or, rather, an assemblage of societies, since the Iberian Peninsula
was divided into four clearly demarcated political units: Castile,
Aragon, Navarre, and Portugal. Each unit varied in size, in population,
and in traditions. But they all had something important in common: for
seven hundred years they represented the Christian resistance to the
Moorish conquest of most of the peninsula, alternately fighting and co-
operating with the Muslim invaders. After seven hundred years the
Christians had absorbed much of the material culture and military
technology of their neighboring rivals. With the fall of the last Moorish
kingdom of Granada in 1492 Iberia was entirely Christian again, divided between Portugal and the relatively recently allied monarchies of

---

[58] Parry, *The Age of Reconnaissance*, p. 96.

Aragon and Castile. While populations of that era were difficult to estimate, it is possible that the Spanish population of 1500 might have been
no more than ten million. Castile incorporated the largest and most
densely populated part of Iberia, with more than 65 percent of the land
area and more than 73 percent of the population.[59]

In many respects Spain was enjoying a golden age in these years.

> The conquest of Granada and the discovery of the America represented
> at once an end and a beginning. While the fall of Granada brought to an
> end the *Reconquista* of Spanish territory, it opened a new phase in
> Castile's long crusade against the Moor—a phase in which the Christian
> banners were borne across the straits and planted on the inhospitable
> shores of Africa. The discovery of the New World also marked the open-
> ing of a new phase—the great epoch of overseas colonization—but at the
> same time it was a natural culmination of a dynamic expansionist period
> in Castilian history, which had begun long before. Both reconquest and
> discovery, which seemed miraculous events to contemporary Spaniards,
> were in reality a logical outcome of the traditions and aspirations of an
> earlier age, on which the seal of success helped to perpetuate at home,
> and project overseas, the ideals, the values and the institutions of me-
> dieval Castile.[60]

Yet the fall of Granada and the discovery of America represented
only two of a number of fateful events of that remarkable year of 1492.
Besides the expulsion of the Moors and the success of Columbus, a
Spaniard, Rodrigo Borgia (1431–1503), became Pope Alexander VI,
thereby giving the Spanish monarchies considerable political leverage
throughout Europe. And, as noted before, Antonio de Nebrija produced his grammar of the Castilian language, thereby emphasizing
Castilian hegemony over the rest of the peninsula as well as the newly
discovered overseas lands and peoples. In presenting his grammar to
Queen Isabella, Nebrija is reputed to have said: "Language, your
majesty, is the ideal weapon of empire."[61] It was a timely gesture for an
aggrandizing monarch, since the newly discovered American lands
would belong exclusively to the Castilian monarchy and would not be
shared with Aragon. While the gesture greatly enhanced the prestige of

---

[59] The figures are taken from the table in Elliott, *Imperial Spain*, p. 25. See also
Richard Herr, *Spain* (New York: Prentice Hall, 1971), pp. 46–7.

[60] Elliott, *Imperial Spain*, pp. 44–5.

[61] Cited in John A. Crow, *Spain: The Root and the Flower: An Interpretation of
Spain and the Spanish People*, 3d rev. ed. (Berkeley: University of California Press, 1985),
p. 151.

Castile, it had little practical consequence. Spaniards from all parts of the peninsula freely migrated to the Americas.

To understand the mentality of both Las Casas and others of his age such as Columbus, Cortés, and Bernal Díaz del Castillo, it is important to recognize what historian Colin M. MacLachlan calls "the intellectual matrix of Spain and its empire."[62] According to MacLachlan, this philosophical matrix "may be divided into three categories: the nature of a monarch's moral and political subordination to divine authority; a ruler's relationship with his subjects; and last, the extent to which legislated law, and proprietary rights conveyed actual authority." The expression "king by the grace of God" implied a certain moral superordinacy that Isabella and Ferdinand had skillfully exploited to glorify themselves and to reinforce their modernizing state in the 15th century. The Catholic monarchs were the sole temporal arbiters of God's will—but they were pragmatic enough to make sure that the church as well as the nobility supported their position. And while the clergy accepted the monarchy as the instrument of God's regency on earth, some individual clergymen felt confident enough to advise their monarch and to criticize royal actions as they saw fit—whether or not it pleased the monarch. Despite its apparent indecision, royal administration worked fairly well. The practical way in which this was achieved derived from a fluid symbiosis between church and state, expressed in the mutual recognition of certain privileges, or *fueros*. In the hierarchical, corporate structure of Spanish society, therefore, every group had its privileges—although not all privileges were equal. Not only was the monarch the sole arbiter of God's will in the temporal sphere, he or she remained the repository of ultimate justice for all. To establish the reality of this concept, Spain fused Christian conversion with Hispanization: to be Spanish was to be Catholic. As historian Richard Herr noted, "The identification of Catholicism with Spanishness penetrated all layers of society."[63] Spain, at considerable cost, would be the principal defender of the faith in Europe, especially after the challenge of Martin Luther's Protestant Reformation. It turned out to be an onerous burden.

Uniformity in church and state required the expulsion of all unconverted Moors and Jews after 1492 and the use of the Royal Inquisition as the litmus test of religious and secular orthodoxy.[64] Moreover, the fall of

---

[62] Colin M. MacLachlan, *Spain's Empire in the New World: The Role of Ideas in Institutional and Social Change* (Berkeley: University of California Press, 1988), p. 1.

[63] Herr, *Spain*, p. 39.

[64] Expulsion of the Jews was periodically carried out among the Christian kingdoms of Iberia as a sort of religious purification rite, but it also had strong political, social,

Granada and the coincident discovery of America reinforced the Spanish royal conviction that Spanish Catholics were superior to all other Catholics. Spain, however, was in many cases the synonym for the kingdom of Castile.[65] When the grandson of Ferdinand and Isabella had himself elected Holy Roman Emperor in 1519—three years after inheriting the Spanish throne—Spanish hegemony within the Catholic sphere became supreme. According to historian John Crow,

> Moor and Jew also gave to Spain that key concept of Spanish Catholicism: religion as a way to nationalism. With no other kind of unity to hold them together the petty Spanish states of medieval times made the banner of the Cross their military, and their national standard. There have been only two successful crusades in history and Spain waged both: the crusade against the Moslem Moors, and the crusade to conquer and Christianize the pagan Indians of the New World. In Spain there never arose a single Protestant Church.[66]

By 1492 the long experience of the *Reconquista* resulted in four clearly delineated but integrally connected interest groups operating within Spanish society: ordinary townsfolk, the military cadres that were sometimes little more than brigands, the regular and secular clergy, and the Christian monarchs supported by an unwieldy cadre of bureaucrats. Good government meant skillful mediation between and among the sometimes conflicting interests of the various competitive entities. But since good government—or the perception of good government—was essential for the well-being of the monarch, Spain spent more than half a century struggling with the notion of a common good and a common justice that satisfied the consciences of warriors, clergymen, and royal advisors. The Spanish struggle for justice was unique in the annals of imperialism. It was a quest to defend Spanish self-interest against all non-Spanish aspirants. Thus what was just for Spaniards was not always just for Indians, and the Crown did not yet have the monopoly of military force in the early years of the establishment of its American empire. Indeed, Spain did not have a standing army anywhere in the Americas until the 18th century. Nor was the American experience easily reconciled with that of Spain and the ancient world or with the magisterial writings of the famous naturalist, Pliny the Elder (AD 25–79), as

---

and economic ramifications. After 1492 about 150,000 Jews were expelled from Spain—considerably fewer than the number of converted Moors expelled later by Philip II.

[65] Jaime Vicens Vives, *Aproximación a la historia de España*, 5th ed. (Barcelona: Vicens Vives, 1968 [1952]), pp. 115–31.

[66] Crow, *Spain*, p. 15.

Gonzalo Fernández de Oviedo (1478–1557)—who had himself been to the Americas—would repeatedly point out in his multivolume opus, *Historia general y natural de las Indias, islas y Tierra Firme del Mar Océano*, written in 1535 [General and natural history of the Indies and Terra Firma of the Ocean Sea].[67]

After 1493 ordinary folk from all parts of the Iberian Peninsula flocked to the Americas. More than two-thirds of the Spaniards who ventured to the New World came from the lower orders of society. Their reasons for going differed greatly. Distance and difficulties, however, did not diminish their strong local attachment to their home region in Spain, as historian Ida Altman has persuasively demonstrated in *Emigrants and Society*. Indeed, to a large extent it can be justly claimed that the Spanish conquest of America was done by the common folk. As Altman perceptively points out:

> Discussion of the many social and occupational groups also has shown the considerable degree of cultural and social homogeneity that characterized the various rankings and groupings of society. Family structure and strategies were similar at all levels of society . . . nobles were closely tied to commoners through business and legal affairs and patron-client, employer-employee, and even kinship relations (consider the illegitimate children who were the products of liaisons between noble men and common women), as well as the face-to-face, ongoing contacts that people who lived in small cities and towns maintained.
>
> The cultural and behavioral homogeneity of Spaniards so notable in the New World setting had its roots in local society in Spain.[68]

The common people, like the freelance conquistadores, went to the Indies—as they had moved around Iberia—to better their lot, improve their status and that of their families, and to serve their patrons and their monarch. Arrival in the Americas sometimes transformed their modest goals, and many immediately took on aspirations of social as well as economic betterment. This may be observed in the frequency with which common folk assumed the title *don*, a deferential term of elevated respect in Spain. Many adventurous immigrants failed in all their goals. Some succeeded beyond their wildest dreams.

The Spanish conquistadores, or freelances, saw the Americas as fertile grounds for continuing the quests of nobility and grandeur that the

---

[67] Gonzalo Fernández de Oviedo y Valdés, *Historia general y natural de las Indias, isles y Tierra Firme del Mar Océano*, ed. Juan Pérez de Tudela (Madrid: Ediciones Atlas, 1959).

[68] Altman, *Emigrants and Society*, pp. 278–9.

fall of Granada and the closing of the Iberian frontier had temporarily terminated. The crown encouraged military activity outside of Spain, and Spaniards like the Pizarros of Trujillo in Extremadura eagerly went to fight elsewhere in Europe. No one expressed the military ideal better than the indefatigable foot soldier of Hernán Cortés, the incomparable Bernal Díaz del Castillo, who declared that they all "went forth to serve God and His Majesty; to bring light to those that dwell in darkness, and to get rich, as all men desire."[69] Serving God was perfectly compatible with the acquisition of wealth and glory, as the case of Las Casas well illustrates. Las Casas reconciled the aggressive pursuit of private wealth with the preaching of the gospel for many years after he came to the Indies. So did his relative Juan de Sosa. The Spanish conquest of the Americas was chaotic and difficult because it was spontaneous, novel, and totally unprecedented, with the rules being arbitrarily designed to fit the continually changing local circumstances. Where applicable, legislation based on the comprehensive *Siete Partidas* of ancient Iberia was introduced, but much of the American experience simply had no precedence in familiar Spanish law or in prevailing Iberian custom.[70] America, therefore, quickly became the locale wherein utopian visions of society would be realized.

At the time of the conquest the Spanish Church, especially the regular orders, was strongly imbued with a dynamic spiritual and intellectual vitality. Drawing much inspiration from Thomas Aquinas, Aristotle, and Erasmus, Franciscans, Dominicans, and Jeronymites saw the Americas as a wonderful new sphere in which to expand the work of God and create vital and viable communities of Christians among the indigenous inhabitants of the Americas.[71] The Franciscans were especially imbued with millennial ideas in the early 16th century.[72] The early success of the church was tempered by the variety of conditions in the Americas and the rapidly changing religious and political situation in

---

[69] Cited in Parry, *The Age of Reconnaissance*, p. 19.

[70] The *Siete Partidas* was the famous codification of Spanish law made by Alfonso X of Leon and Castile toward the end of the 13th century. It was updated about every hundred years. See E. N. Van Kleffens, *Hispanic Law until the End of the Middle Ages* (Edinburgh: Edinburgh University Press, 1968).

[71] Crow, *Spain*, p. 159; Brading, *The First America*, pp. 102–27.

[72] Millennial ideas arose from general apocalyptic belief that after a thousand years Christ would return to earth, and a period, presumably of another thousand years, of peace, happiness, and perfect Christianity would prevail prior to the end of the world. For an extensive discussion, see Phelan, *The Millennial Kingdom*.

Europe, especially after the rise of Protestantism.[73] Although there was
no uniform position taken by the church, mostly it did reject the more
extreme inclinations of natural law that permeated the legal training of
Spanish bureaucrats. In the Americas the church worked hand in hand
with the Crown. It had no choice. By 1492 the Spanish Church was the
influential and highly useful spiritual arm of the Spanish State. The
Spanish monarch controlled both the regular and the secular clergy
(except the newly constituted Jesuit order).[74] But there was benevolent
reciprocity. If the Crown controlled the church, the church could, and
did, influence Crown policy. Clergymen remained important advisers
to the Crown, and in the Americas the cross and the sword marched
harmoniously together: churchmen frequently became bureaucrats and
some, like Cardinal Cisneros, served the state for very long periods. No
one in the early decades of the 16th century, however, exploited the relation between church and state better than Bartolomé de las Casas.

Of course the Crown tried to impose order on the rapidly moving situation in the Indies. Given the long distances overseas and the modes of
transportation and communication, which was not easy. Much of
Spain's administrative policy in the first half of the 16th century can be
seen as an attempt to establish royal control and avoid the problems that
confronted royal administration in Iberia. If Isabella had casually
granted enormous feudal powers to Columbus before he sailed for the
New World, she was careful to cut him down to size when he returned
to Spain with the surprising news that he had indeed discovered vast
new lands and uncounted new peoples for Castile and for himself. The
strategy that the Castilian Crown employed against Columbus was con-
sistent throughout much of the century: the Americas would be a
Castilian royal patrimony and would be administered as such.[75] Autonomy was anathema. A series of legislative measures progressively established effective administration in what Castile regarded as newly found
royal lands—not a reconquered domain already settled with Spaniards
in politically pesky cities as in southern Spain. In 1493 Ferdinand and
Isabella got the pope to divide the world between Spain and Portugal,
but they were also intelligent enough to reinforce whatever moral force

---

[73] Gibson, *Spain in America* (New York: Harper & Row, 1966), pp. 68–89; Eric
Wolfe, *Sons of the Shaking Earth* (Chicago: University of Chicago Press, 1959), chapter 8.

[74] Although founded by Ignatius de Loyola, a Basque nobleman, the Society of
Jesus, approved by Pope Paul II in 1540, was directed from Rome and subordinate solely
to the pope.

[75] Gibson, *Spain in America*, pp. 90–111.

was supplied by the papal ruling with a secular bilateral agreement between the two states, signed at Tordesillas. In 1500 Isabella had Columbus free the Indians he had brought back to Spain with him as slaves, declaring them to be her vassals and therefore exempt from enslavement. In 1512 the Laws of Burgos sought to ameliorate the material condition of Indians in *encomienda,* insisting that they be adequately fed and provided with Christian instruction. The Requirement of 1514, a compromise document designed to mediate between evangelists and labor-short colonists, declared that only warring Indians could be enslaved, and that before each military campaign the Spanish should read a proclamation in Latin informing the Indians that they had resisted peaceful intercourse, thereby giving the Spanish just cause for war. The result of the war would be the enslavement of surviving males.[76] The New Laws of 1542 represented the most extensive application of the royal prerogative. The preamble read:

> **Whereas** one of the most principal things in which the *Audiencias* are to serve us is in taking very special care for the good treatment of the Indians and the preservation of them: **We do command** that they inform themselves always of the excesses and ill-treatments that are or were done to said Indians by governors or particular persons, and in what manner the ordinances and instructions that have been given them, and that for the good treatment of them are hereby given, have been and are observed, and in so far as those instructions may have been exceeded or may in future be exceeded, said *Audiencias* shall take care to remedy those treatments by punishing the guilty with all severity and rigour consonant with justice.[77]

Although it did not succeed entirely, it demonstrated clearly that the Crown's preoccupation with justice for the American Indians was as much a form of imperial self-preservation as any altruistic need to protect its vassals.[78] Yet the important point is that the Spanish Crown, for whatever reasons, remained conscious of its corporate obligation to protect the interests of the populations that Isabella had considered in 1493 to be her new vassals.

---

[76] It is important to remember that as late as the Napoleonic Wars of the 19th century their captors regularly enslaved captives of wars in the Mediterranean.

[77] *The New Laws,* p. xii. See also, Chapter 3, p. 95 in this edition.

[78] MacLachlan, *Spain's Empire,* pp. 58–60.

The Americas in the Age of Las Casas

Spaniards of the 16th century, including Columbus and Las Casas, failed to appreciate the enormous variety in social and political organization of the indigenous peoples of the Americas. The various reports submitted, beginning with that of Columbus, did try to describe a highly variegated structure ranging from the large, complex empires of the Aztecs and Incas in Central Mexico and the Andean highlands to nomadic bands of people on the great plains of North and South America. Father Ramón Pané himself attested several times to his frustration with the several languages with which he had to communicate:

> The Lord Admiral [Christopher Columbus] told me then that the language then spoken in the province of Magdalena [or] Macorís was different from the other one and was not understood throughout the country [Hispaniola]. Nonetheless, [he told me that] I should go to live with another principal *cacique* called Guarionex, lord of many people, because his language was understood throughout the land. And it is indeed true that I said to the Lord Governor Christopher Columbus: "Sir, how is it that Your Lordship wishes me to go live with Guarionex, knowing no language other than that of Macorís? Let Your Lordship grant me some Nuhuirey people, who later became Christians and knew both languages, to accompany me." He granted this request and told me to take with me whoever pleased me.[79]

The differences on Hispaniola were multiplied a thousand times on the mainland. Nevertheless, Europeans all tended to homogenize the Indians and treat them as one large, intellectually and technologically inferior community.

Las Casas referred frequently to specific numbers throughout his writings, and we shall return to those later. But how densely populated were the central regions of the Americas in 1492? Producing reliable figures for populations existing more than five hundred years ago is not an easy task. There was no proper way to do a head count or even a household estimate. Moreover, the arriving Spaniards were relatively few compared with the populations they initially encountered. Even with the later organized transatlantic slave trade with its bottleneck, or chokepoint, on the ships of the Atlantic Ocean, the estimates varied enormously from one author to the other.[80] It was much more difficult

---

[79] Fray Ramón Pané, *An Account of the Antiquities of the Indians*, pp. 33–4.

[80] Paul E. Lovejoy, "The Volume of the Atlantic Slave Trade: A Synthesis," in *Journal of African History* 23:4 (1982): 473–501.

to estimate populations scattered over millions of square miles. With the indigenous population, some extremely interesting but widely diverse figures have been produced over the last half-century. Anthropologist and geographer William Denevan, in *The Native Populations of the Americas in 1492*, provided some of the most thoughtful evaluation of the various estimates of populations at the time of the conquest.[81] The range of total populations for all the Americas falls between 8.4 million and more than 100 million. While the lower range may seem somewhat modest, the higher figures appear to defy credulity. It is inconceivable that the Americas were as densely populated as Europe, Africa, or Asia.

Yet if no consensus exists on the exact population of the Americas, there is better agreement on two important aspects: the spatial distribution of the population and its catastrophic decline after the arrival of the Europeans. Certainly everyone agreed that the densest population concentrations were found in the Nahuatl-speaking controlled central valley of Mexico and the Inca Empire of highland Peru. The lowest concentrations were at the northern and southern extremes of the hemisphere and the Brazilian bulge of South America. Similarly, there is agreement on the demise of the indigenous population after 1492. As Denevan indicates:

> Despite the disagreement about the size of the New World Indian population, there is little doubt about the massive and rapid drop in that population in the 16th century. The discovery of America was followed by possibly the greatest demographic disaster in the history of the world. And unlike past population crises in Europe and Asia from epidemics, wars, and climate, where full recovery did occur, the Indian population of America recovered slowly, partially, and in highly modified form. In 1650 the native population numbered only about 4,000,000 south of the United States . . . [Most] Indian cultures have become extinct or nearly so. Many of those groups that have survived remain threatened with extinction for much the same reasons as in the 16th century: disease, inhumanity, misguided "salvation," and racial and cultural mixing to the point of non-recognition.[82]

The quantity of the New World population is intrinsically important since it correlates with other aspects of society, economy, and culture.

---

[81] William M. Denevan, *The Native Population of the Americas in 1492* (Madison: The University of Wisconsin Press, 1976). See also Bakewell, *Latin America*, pp. 151–3; and Pedro Julio Santiago, Julio G. Campillo Pérez, and Carlos Doral, *El primer Santiago de América, 1495–1995* (Santo Domingo, Dominican Republic: Academia de Historia, 1997), pp. 167–8.

[82] Denevan, *Native Population*, p. 7.

Denevan eventually accepted "a range of 43,000,000 to 72,000,000" for all the Americas.[83]

But that range still allows for a population of close to six million for the Caribbean—and that seems excessive in light of the other known factors of 15th-century Caribbean society and culture.[84]

Whatever the actual population at the time of the conquest, all indigenous American societies were essentially shattered culturally, demographically, politically, and economically by the arrival of the Europeans. Much of the shattering was done in warfare, as Las Casas described with numbing monotony. But warfare alone would not have decimated so large a population in so relatively short a time. Far more Indians succumbed to the ravages of unfamiliar epidemic diseases than to the swords and dogs of the invading Spanish warriors. Although the inadvertent introduction of unfamiliar diseases also had a lethal effect in parts of Africa and in Polynesia, nowhere was the effect as devastating as throughout the Americas. Much of the shattering derived from the myriad unforeseen circumstances accompanying the revolutionary changes in epidemiology, ecology, politics, and society. The implications for all the American host societies of the arrival of the Europeans proved transcendental. The biological and cultural consequences were incalculable after 1492.[85] To arrive at the decline observed at the end of the 16th century, it was possible that mortality rates among some indigenous communities might have reached 25 percent per year. More significant, morbidity rates would have ranged between 50 and 100 percent. With morbidity rates of such destructive magnitude, many communities simply could not function at all. Under such conditions, social cohesion and cultural traditions definitely could not be maintained. Some native peoples did survive of course—but they survived in a totally new world, in a totally new environment of newly organized villages, cities, haciendas, mines, and plantations. Many survivors were no longer biologically or culturally Indian, but often mestizos, the offspring of the union of conquerors and conquered. Nor was the metamorphosis solely demographic. Native inhabitants everywhere had to confront the complete restructuring of all the basic institutions of religion, com-

---

[83] Ibid., p. 291.

[84] See Samuel M. Wilson, ed., *The Indigenous People of the Caribbean* (Gainesville: University Press of Florida, 1997); Carl Ortwin Sauer, *The Early Spanish Main* (Berkeley: University of California Press, 1969); Troy S. Floyd, *The Columbus Dynasty in the Caribbean, 1492–1526* (Albuquerque, NM: University of New Mexico Press, 1973).

[85] See Alfred W. Crosby, *The Columbian Exchange: Biological and Cultural Consequences of 1492* (Westport, CT: Greenwood Press, 1972).

merce, politics, and social organization and worldview. All this destroyed their cultural cohesiveness and challenged their concepts of themselves and their world. In some cases and in some places the transformation was rapid. In other cases the changes were more slowly drawn out. Everywhere, however, change, either by imposition or by adaptation, was the order of the day.

> The Indian before the Conquest had been a cultivator, a seed planter. The conquering Spaniard became a mining entrepreneur, a producer of commercial crops, a rancher, a merchant. The strategic economic relationship of the pre-Conquest period united Indian peasant and Indian lord, tribute-producer and tribute-consumer. The goal of the Indian noble was to consume wealth commensurate with his social position. The Spanish colonist, however, labored for different ends. He wanted to convert wealth and labor into salable goods—into gold and silver, hides and wool, wheat and sugar cane. No Spaniard could count himself wealthy as a mere recipient of loads of maize, pieces of jade, or cacao beans. Wealth to him meant wealth invested in Spanish goods, capital multiplying miraculously in the process of exchange. He had not braved the hardships of the Indies merely to come into the inheritance of his Indian predecessor; he wanted to organize and press the human resources under his command, to pay his debts, to enlarge his estate, to take his place among the other men grown rich and powerful in the new utopia.[86]

Yet the indigenous populations did not unilaterally feel the profound changes wrought by the conquest. Spain and the rest of Europe—as well as Africa and Asia—would also be dramatically affected by the incorporation of the Americas into Castile. Increased volumes of precious metals and expanded trade altered international relations. By the time Las Casas died in 1566, Spain had received more than £28,000,000 worth of gold and silver bullion from the Americas.[87] American silver would help revolutionize the economies of Western Europe.[88] Although Las Casas continued to protest the ill treatment of the Indians, he could not have held out much hope for the success of his plan of

---

[86] Wolf, *Sons of the Shaking Earth*, p. 176.

[87] R. Trevor Davies, *The Golden Century of Spain* (New York: St. Martin's Press, 1967), pp. 299–300. The total does not include illegal imports, calculated at between 10 and 50 percent.

[88] See Ralph Davis, *The Rise of the Atlantic Economies* (Ithaca, NY: Cornell University Press, 1973), pp. 1–156; Philip D. Curtin, *The Rise and Fall of the Plantation Complex: Essays in Atlantic History* (Cambridge: Cambridge University Press, 1990), pp. 17–91.

religious utopias productively supporting the crown of Castile. The
Spaniards came to the Americas seeking gold. They found it in large
quantities, and they were determined to have it whatever the human
cost. The deposits of American silver were even greater than the deposits
of gold. The indigenous populations, of course, would pay most of the
frightful human cost to put those metals in commercial circulation.

Las Casas and the Utopian View of the Americas

The *Brevísima Relación* provides an excellent insight into not only the
mind of Las Casas but also his literary style. Yet, the full measure of the
man cannot be garnered from this single work. Las Casas has represented many things to many people: idealist, ethnographer, *indigenista*,
antifeudalist, anti-Spanish propagandist, ideologue, and anticolonialist.
Some views derive from looking at the court politics of Las Casas. Other
views derive from his various writings. And many come from the con-
text of the times and the changing symbolic significance of what Las
Casas stood for at that particular moment in time. Indeed, one indication of this complex reception of Las Casas is illustrated by the pattern
of foreign translations of works by Las Casas. An early account mention-
ing Las Casas appeared in 1565 in Venice, and an Italian printed version of the *Brevísima Relación* came out as early as 1616. Various
versions appeared in English and Dutch after the 1580s.[89] Clearly Las
Casas' writings were a tool in the anti-Spanish conflicts being conducted
by both the Dutch and the English at the time. This reflects two inter-
related aspects of Las Casas and his work—his Christian humanist, pro-
Indian advocacy and his potentially anti-imperial, anticolonial political
posture. In any case, Las Casas' views underwent a progressive evolution, although he never wavered from the basic concept that he proposed in the second decade of the 16th century, when he became
convinced of the intrinsic justice of Indian equality and liberation.
Moreover, like all great writers such as William Shakespeare
(1564–1616) and Miguel de Cervantes (1547–1616), the written work
had a certain special quality that resonated down through the ages. The
present translator, Andrew Hurley, has provided some extremely useful
notes on the literary style, and several distinguished scholars including
the long-serving Spanish philologist, Ramon Menéndez Pidal

---

[89] Benjamin Keen, *Essays in the Intellectual History of Colonial Latin America*
(Boulder, CO: Westview Press, 1998), pp. 79–83.

(1869–1968), have attacked both Las Casas' language and his personality.[90] Las Casas, after 1514, was a man possessed. As such he wrote in the strong, compelling, polemical manner designed to sway the reader. Hyperbole came easily and irony laced his narration. His principal credential, he often repeated, was his extensive personal experience in the Indies. He wrote about what he had witnessed or heard directly from those who had themselves witnessed, and he claims no one else could do so with comparable authority.[91]

Much like Columbus after his third voyage, Las Casas regarded the Indians as perfect natural specimens living in a veritable paradise:

> All these universal and infinite peoples, . . . God created to be a simple people, altogether without subtlility, malice, or duplicity, excellent in obedience, most loyal to their native lords and to the Christians whom they serve; the most humble, most patient, meekest and most pacific, slowest to take offence and most tranquil in demeanor, least quarrelous, least querulous, most lacking in rancor and hatreds or desire for vengeance of all the peoples of the earth.[92]

Statements like these are not easily reconciled with the repeated descriptions of incessant warfare—in some of which Las Casas himself was engaged before he saw the light—on the Caribbean islands and on the Central American mainland. Throughout the centuries of conquest and colonization, the indigenous population did not accept their conquest without spirited resistance. Whether slow to revenge or not, Indians destroyed the initial settlement established by Columbus at La Isabela on northern Hispaniola and repeatedly wiped out fledgling Christian communities along the Venezuelan coast. They did not resign themselves benignly to their fate. Wars and uprisings plagued the Spanish administrations, from the early revolts of Higuey and Hatuey in Hispaniola and Cuba in the early 1500s to the major insurrection of Tupac Amaru in Upper Peru in the late 1700s. Indeed, the Caribs in the eastern Antillean islands all but made Spanish settlement impossible there and resisted the French and English with grim determination in Martinique, Guadeloupe, St. Lucia, and St. Vincent. Some of their descendants continue to live in St. Vincent, and others were deported in

---

[90] Ramon Menéndez Pidal, *El padre Las Casas: Su doble personalidad* (Madrid: Espasa-Calpe, 1963). This publication stimulated enormous debate. See Friede and Keen, *Las Casas*, pp. 612–3; and Keen, *Essays*, especially pp. 1–69.

[91] The same appeal to eye-witnessing as an essential dimension of credibility or authenticity may be noticed in the history by Bernal Díaz del Castillo.

[92] All quotations from Las Casas' *Brevísima Relación* are from this edition of Andrew Hurley's translation.

earlier centuries to form the Garifuna communities in contemporary Belize, Honduras, Nicaragua, and Guatemala.

If Las Casas' description of Indian societies tends to be overdrawn, so are his figures for the local populations. Of one of the kingdoms of Hispaniola he wrote:

> It is five leagues wide and sometimes eight and even ten, and has highlands in one part and another. It is crossed by above thirty thousand rivers and streams, among them twelve as large as the Ebro and Duero and Guadalquivir; and all of the rivers that flow down from a mountain which is to the west, which number twenty and twenty-five thousand, are most extraordinarily rich in gold. In that mountain, or mountain range, lies the province of Cibao, from which comes down that gold high in carats which is so famed here.

Neither the actual number of rivers nor the recovered volume of gold conformed to the exaggerated statement of the well-intentioned priest. Indeed, the early Spanish colonists, disappointed by the exploratory results in Hispaniola, quickly spread out to the neighboring islands in quest of gold and other forms of wealth. The Caribbean region never proved "extraordinarily rich" in precious metals, and only with the conquest of Mexico and Peru did bullion pour into Spain as well as the rest of Europe in unprecedented proportions.

Numbers were certainly not Las Casas' forte. Of the populations of Jamaica and Puerto Rico he wrote:

> On those two aforesaid islands there had once been above six hundred thousand souls, and I believe above a million, and yet today there are no more than two hundred persons on each, all having perished without faith and without sacraments.

In 1492 the population of neither island scarcely exceeded the tens of thousands and the decline, while exceedingly steep, was probably not as dramatic as Las Casas indicated. The same applies for his description of the devastation of Nicaragua:

> In this wise they have taken from that province above five hundred thousand souls of Indians made slaves, though being truly as free as I. And from the hellish wars that the Spaniards have waged upon them, and from the abominable captivity in which they are cast, more again have died than another five hundred and six hundred thousand persons until this day, and still today they are being slain. In a space of fourteen years, all of these devastations have been done. And today, in all that province of Nicaragua there are probably not above four or five thousand persons . . .

In the final analysis, what was at stake was not the mathematical accuracy of Las Casas' account but the essentially Christian humanist purpose for which he wrote. Las Casas might have employed hyperbolic language, but he did not imagine the callous and casual ways in which Spanish invaders abused the indigenous populations and arbitrarily appropriated their lands. The precipitous decline of the indigenous population was dramatically self-evident by 1530, although the reasons were far more complex than the simple Spanish cruelty that Las Casas repeatedly described. Although historians have copied his numbers and repeated his descriptions, they have also been impressed by his energetic devotion to the cause of justice for the oppressed peoples of the Americas. And he couched his language in terms of fundamental human rights, insisting that all the peoples of the world were equal in the sight of God and deserved equal treatment, irrespective of their material conditions. In this respect his position exceeded those of even the most benevolent of his compatriots who supported civil rights for the local people, anticipating that they would therefore become good Spanish subjects. To Las Casas in his radical later days, indigenous rights were in every way equivalent to Spanish rights—and took precedence over the latter. His argument was that the Spanish could not entirely disregard the legitimate natural rights of the indigenous population simply because they were not Christians.

Indeed, even earlier, when he was writing the *Brevísima Relación*, Las Casas implied that the royal agreement to develop parts of the Americas was obtained through duplicity and the monarch was ignorant of the process and conduct of his colonizers:

> In the year 1526, through deceit and certain malicious persuasions of our lord the king (for men of evil intentions have always worked to conceal from him the harms and perditions that God and the people's souls and the king's estate suffer in those lands of the Indies), the king did give over and concede a great realm, much greater than all of Spain, which is the kingdom of Venezuela, with its entire rule and governance and jurisdiction, to certain merchants of Germany, with a certain capitulation and agreement or assent that he made with them. These men, having made *entrada* with three hundred men or above, found countless nations as gentle and meek as lambs, like the others (or even more so) who were generally to be found in all parts of the Indies before the Spaniards did them such great harm. These men entered into those lands, then, with more, I do think, incomparable cruelty than any of the tyrants that we have spoken of, and more unreasonably and furiously than the most bloodthirsty tigers and ravening wolves and lions. For with more eagerness and more blind and wrathful avarice, and with much more exquisite skillfulness and ingenuity in obtaining and robbing silver and gold than all those who went before, and putting aside all fear of God and the king and the shame of humankind, and forgetting that they were mortal men,

and with more freedom and brazenness and daring than any others, they
took possession of all the jurisdiction of the land.

Las Casas never deviated from his conscience and his principles.
Through his prolific writings and his tireless personal intervention he
did effectively influence the course of Spanish-Indian relations in the
New World. Moreover, he gave the example that one determined person could make a difference—most significantly in the papal pro-
nouncement of 1537 declaring the Indians to be rational, as well as in
the promulgation of the New Laws of 1542 modifying Indian servitude
throughout the Americas. Largely due to Las Casas, Spain never re-
treated officially from the position adopted by Queen Isabella that the
newly discovered populations were her vassals for whom the monarchy
of Castile had some responsibility. But Las Casas was far less successful
at personal administration either at Cumaná or in Nicaragua. Today
that matters less. Las Casas was a superb propagandist and quite astute
at court politics. His writings and his actions may have agitated the royal
court, but he had the respect of the monarchs. In his fading years Philip
II ordered that he be provided adequate lodgings at court as long as he
needed them. Nevertheless, the court was less diligent in facilitating the
dissemination of the ideas of Las Casas. Much of his writings, although
available in manuscript form, were never published until centuries after
he died. Despite this, the *Brevísima Relación* ranks among the most
widely translated and diffused texts in modern history. Enemies of the
Spanish loved it, of course. It also circulated throughout the Spanish
American empire, inflaming the political passions of succeeding generations of supporters and detractors down through the ages. And it did
this for a simple but powerful reason. The cause of justice for all consti-
tutes one of the fundamental pursuits of every good society. Whenever
and wherever one group oppresses another there will be room for the
sentiments of Las Casas. As long as colonizers exploit and subordinate
the colonized the writings of Las Casas will remain vitally relevant. As
long as one group will arbitrarily appropriate the land and property of
another, as still happens throughout the world today, the arguments of
Las Casas will resonate loudly and repeatedly. As long as all people are
not equally free or lack respect in their own land, the familiar passion of
Las Casas will inform the passions of contemporary pleas. Justice, freedom, and dignity are universal traits that never lose their currency.
These sentiments permeated the frequently repeated arguments of Bartolomé de las Casas. And that is why all who strive for those noble
causes such as Las Casas will never be forgotten.

Franklin W. Knight
Johns Hopkins University

A Note on the Text and the Translation

If, as I believe, the past is another country, then Bartolomé de las Casas' *Account, Much Abbreviated, of the Destruction of the Indies* lies at two countries' remove from us in the English-speaking world today, for there is first the other country of the Spanish language and then the other country of the mid-16th century. For a translator into English, the inherent "otherness" of Spanish is easier to bring home to readers than the less-often-considered "otherness" lent by that immense distance in time. Speaking personally (and of course I am speaking as a translator, not as a historian; it would be interesting to put the question to a historian of the late Middle Ages and early Renaissance), the worldview of the early 16th century is far more alien to me than the worldview implied by the Spanish language. In a sense, even the way "logic" worked then is different from "logic" in our day; the conclusions that seemed so apparent, so "natural," to a person of the 16th century are sometimes not apparent at all to one immersed in the mindset of the late 20th and early 21st centuries. Consider Las Casas' unconsidered monarchism, his fierce Catholicism, which leads him to demonize the Lutherans, his "logic" of illness among the pearl divers, and his suggestion (bizarre to us today) that the native peoples of the Caribbean be saved by importing African slaves to replace them.[1] What passes for "enlightenment" in one age may seem—worse than misguided—sheer barbarity in another, and one age's political correctness (not to mention the elements of courtesy and good manners) is another age's disgusting bigotry and offense. The shared knowledge of one age can be lost to the next, and

---

[1] Although in the *Brevísima Relación* Las Casas drips irony on the Spaniards who "cared" for the souls of the Indians by sending them to die in the mines, the remedy for this practice, which he suggests in some of his writings, was not without its irony, either, as Jorge Luis Borges reminds readers in the first lines of his story "The Dreadful Redeemer Lazarus Morel," in the volume *A Universal History of Iniquity*: "In 1517 [*sic*], Fray Bartolomé de las Casas, feeling great pity for the Indians who grew worn and lean in the drudging infernos of the Antillean gold mines, proposed to Emperor Charles V that Negroes be brought to the isles of the Caribbean, so that *they* might grow worn and lean in the drudging infernos of the Antillean gold mines. [What an] odd variant on the species *philanthropist*."

geography itself—not to mention cosmology—can change immensely. (In 1492, we should remember, a whole "new world" was "discovered"; for many things found in this new place, there were not even any words. It is hard for us today to feel, deep within us, how truly astounding this discovery was, and the effect it had on complacent Europe.) The meanings of words shift over time; new words come into the language, old words fade away, and the way words are combined in "standard" discourse changes unpredictably.

And so for historical texts, even more than for the "normal" foreign-language texts (an interesting fiction, that), which require translation, the translator must make hard choices: Shall I update the language? Shall I "archaize" my text? Shall I smooth out the rough contours of the syntax of four centuries ago or leave it in a state that most modern readers would consider chaotic or at least convoluted? Shall I smooth out and soften language that is too "rough" or somehow offensive for today? (That is, are Las Casas' *indios* to be Indians, or shall they be "native peoples" or some similar locution?) Shall I "correct" attitudes that today seem unenlightened? And shall I do so silently or in footnotes or endnotes? How shall I convey mere "information" that was accessible, shared in one age but lost to the next: By interpolation of explanation into the text? In notes? In a foreword or afterword? Shall I not supply it at all but rather leave it to interested readers to ferret it out for themselves? (Will readers know or recognize what they don't know?)

The choices are not easy, as I say, and whichever way one takes, the path is fraught with perils—not to mention that lurking along the side of the road are people, readers, ready to criticize whatever decisions, whatever strategies one finally adopts. (Some hate footnotes, some find them helpful; some hate words such as "mankind" and the generic "he," while others feel using gender-inclusive language is rewriting history.) The best thing—perhaps the only thing—the translator can do is make his or her choices consciously, with as much awareness as he (in this case) or she can muster, and then openly disclose those choices to the readers of the translated text, trusting that those readers will at least acknowledge that there is no "one way," no one *good* way, to solve these unsolvable dilemmas.

In the text that follows, I have preserved Las Casas' repetitive and somewhat rambling style while at the same time bringing his Spanish more or less into line with "standard" English syntax—arranging the parts of the sentence the way English "expects" those parts to be arranged. The syntax, then, will seem relatively "natural," I believe, although a bit antiquated, while the lexicon may not seem natural at all, though I believe it will be perfectly understandable.

With respect to that lexicon, I have not updated the language and, in fact, have decided that this translation shall include no word that entered the English language after about 1560—that is, before Shakespeare, before the King James Bible (1611), before the expansion and, of course, incredible "enriching" or blossoming of the language (in terms of both lexicon and style) that those two "authors" brought about. (I have provided footnotes where the meaning of certain archaic usages might be confused with the modern meaning: "complexion" for "constitution," for example.) What this choice means in practice is that I have not been able to use the words "settle," "settlement," or "populate" for the Spaniards' colonizing efforts but instead have had to use "inhabit." I have not been able to say "horrendous" or "horrible," though "terrible" has been permitted. I have not been able to say "shark" or "barracuda." All those words entered English later than the assumed time of my translation. If there was more than one word that might work for my translation (though this rarely happened, since the English lexicon of the early 16th century was much smaller than even fifty years later), I have generally chosen the word that has the more "biblical" ring to it. In this, I believe I am following Las Casas' lead, since as a friar in a religious order he quotes or alludes to Bible passages several times. (Clearly, he is making comparisons with the biblical mistreatments of the Jews.) Presented with a choice between "docile" and "meek," that is, I have chosen "meek"; between the Indians fleeing into the "*woods*" and the "*wilderness*," I have chosen "wilderness," for a certain sense of parallelism with Old Testament events and the words the King James redactors used a few years later to present them.

Obviously I have been forced by my lexical choices to use "British" rather than "American" spelling, since British spelling was all there was in the 16th century; I have not, though, attempted to recreate all the varieties of spelling that appear in the late-medieval English texts of the 15th and early 16th centuries, before spelling was regularized. By the same respect, I have chosen not to bring the text into line with more modern word-choices intended to promote nonprejudiced use of the language. I follow 16th-century usage and call the Antilles the "Indies," and call the indigenous peoples of the Americas "Indians."

In formulating this translation strategy and carrying it out, I have not pretended to myself that this text might have been produced by a native 16th-century English speaker or by a 16th-century native English-language translator from the Spanish; the analogy I might use is that this text, in its lexicon and choice of words, its syntax, and its "naivete," might have been produced by someone learning the English language *of* the 16th century *in* the 16th century—someone from the 21st century taking a time-machine ride, for instance, or a 16th-century Spanish speaker. Many of the recondite words and particular turns of phrase that a native English speaker of a certain education and class might have used are not here; words that have disappeared in the 400-year evolution of the language are generally not here, though it has been impossible, as I have noted above, to avoid obsolete meanings of still-existing words. Again: this text does not pretend to recreate the exact manner of speaking or writing of that time, but it is a text that *might* have been produced then (certainly there are no lexical anachronisms from the 19th or 20th century), and its vocabulary is authentic. Notwithstanding that authenticity, the text "knows," as I know, that it is a translation; thus, it is an *approximation* to a text and to a time.

I have felt that this approach was necessary in order to restore to Las Casas a certain kind of otherness—the otherness of a historical moment when what he said was challenging, shocking, and controversial in the extreme—which, in the course of time and fame, he has lost. Bartolomé de las Casas holds a place in the canon of human-rights literature in English; his name, what he stood for, and what he argued against are well known by most "educated" readers in English today. And thus we feel that he—like Dante, like Freud, like de Tocqueville, like the brothers Grimm, or like the writers and tellers of the tales of the *1001 Nights*—is "one of us," even if we've never read him. He, and they, form part of the invisible background of our culture, and we are complacent about them. In order for us to truly *read* them, one of two things then probably needs to happen: either we need to come to them with new eyes, or they need to be "made new." This translation, by pushing Las Casas back into his own past, by refusing to update the lexicon or predigest his sentences and his ideas, by showing the *limitations* of his vision (those "Indians"!) as well as its enlightenedness and modernity, attempts to make Las Casas new for a new generation of readers. His prose is not meant here to seem "familiar"; the paradoxical hope is that by seeming "old" or "other" it will also seem new and perhaps even challenging, shocking, and controversial, and will be read for what it actually says, not what we think—because we've "heard so much about him"—it says. Perhaps in that way—because we must strain to hear it against the background noise of our contemporary culture—Las Casas' message can be heard by new readers in this new world that Las Casas was striving to make *good* as well as merely new. And if it is heard, then perhaps we will be able to see that the ills that Las Casas argued and struggled against—atrocities in the service of empire, horrors (whether against human beings or the environment) perpetrated in the quest for riches—are still with us today, and perhaps we will be able to continue fighting his good fight for our fellow human beings and for the moral health of our societies.

For this translation, I have followed the text of André Saint-Lu's tenth edition of the *Brevísima relación de la destruición de las Indias* (Madrid: Ediciones Cátedra [Letras Hispanas series], 1996). In his text, Saint-Lu modernizes most of Las Casas' irregular spelling, but he does not modernize or regularize the syntax or disambiguate ambiguities (as of personal pronouns) in the text.

Andrew Hurley
San Juan, Puerto Rico
2001–2003

Some Earlier English Translations of Bartolomé de las Casas' *Brevísima relación de la destruición de las Indias*

The Spanish Colonie, or Briefe Chronicle of the Acts and gestes of the Spaniardes in the West Indies, Called the Newe World, for the space of xl yeere, translated by "M.M.S." (London, 1583).

A briefe narration of the destruction of the Indies by the Spaniards, translated ? (London, 1625).

The Tears of the Indians: Being an Historical and true Account of the Cruel Massacres and Slaughters of above Twenty Millions of innocent People, Committed by the Spaniards in the Islands of Hispaniola, Cuba, Jamaica, &c. As also, in the Continent of Mexico, Peru, & other Places of the West-Indies, to the total destruction of those Countries, Written in Spanish by Casaus, an Eye-witness of those things, and made English by J.P., translated by John Phillips (London, 1656).

Tears of the Indians, by Bartolomé de las Casas, and The Hope of Las Casas, by Sir Arthur Helps. Introduction by Lewis Hanke. (Williamstown, MA: John Lilburne Company. 1970).

The Devastation of the Indies: A Brief Account, translated by Herma Briffault (Baltimore: Johns Hopkins University Press, 1992).

In Defense of the Indians: The Defense of the Most Reverend Lord, Don Fray Bartolomé de las Casas, of the Order of Preachers, late Bishop of Chiapa, against the persecutors and slanderers of the peoples of the New World discovered across the seas, translated and edited by Stafford Poole, foreword by Martin E. Marty (DeKalb: Northern Illinois University Press, ca. 1992).

A Short Account of the Destruction of the Indies, translated and edited by Nigel Griffin, with an introduction by Anthony Pagden (London/New York: Penguin Classics, 1992).

———

Anthologies of Las Casas' Writings

Bartolomé de las Casas; A Selection of His Writings, translated and edited by George Sanderlin (New York: Knopf, 1971).

History of the Indies, translated and edited by Andrée Collard (New York: Harper & Row, 1971).

Indian Freedom: The Cause of Bartolomé de las Casas, 1484–1566: A Reader. Translations and notes by Francis Patrick Sullivan (Kansas City, MO: Sheed & Ward, 1995).

An Account, Much Abbreviated, of the Destruction of the Indies
Bartolomé de las Casas

Argument of the Present Epitome[1]

All the things that have taken place in the Indies, both since their marvellous discovery and those first years when Spaniards first went out to
them to remain for some time, and then in the process thereafter down
to these our own days, have been so extraordinary and so in no wise[2] to
be believed by any person who did not see them, that they seem to have
clouded and laid silence and oblivion upon all those other deeds, however bold and dauntless they might be, that in centuries past were ever
seen and heard in this world. Among these terrible things are the
slaughters and ruins of innocent people, the depopulations[3] of villages,
provinces, and kingdoms in those Indies, and many other acts of no less
heinous and abominable character. Respecting these acts, the Bishop
don Fray Bartolomé de las Casas or Casaus, after having been made a
friar,[4] came to Court to inform the Emperor our lord, who had ever
looked with approval upon all these things. And Las Casas, chancing
also to narrate these deeds to divers persons who did not know of them,
caused a manner of ecstasy and suspension of spirit in his hearers with
his narration, and he was begged and importuned to put some of them,
briefly, into writing. And so he did, but seeing some years later many insensible[5] men, brought by their covetousness and ambition to fall from
the estate of humanity and led by their wicked deeds to reprobate mind

---

[1] Summary, condensed account.

[2] "Way," as in the modern term "likewise," meaning "in a similar way."

[3] Devastations, wiping out all the people from the villages.

[4] This was in 1540, at the court of Emperor Charles V (1500–1558), who was Holy
Roman Emperor from 1519 to 1556 and king of Spain as Charles from 1516 to 1556.
Charles was the son of Philip I of Castile and the grandson of Ferdinand and Isabella.

[5] Insensitive, hard of heart and spirit.

1

(as the Bible sayeth), and not content with the treasons and mischief
that they have committed, depopulating that realm with exquisite forms
of cruelty, but yet importuning the king for licence and authority to
commit those acts yet again, and others yet worse (if worse there might
be)—, that same Las Casas has determined to present this summary of
that other treatise touching this matter that he once wrote to the Prince
our lord,[6] so that His Highness might be led, by reading it, to refuse
those petitions. And it has seemed to Las Casas meet that these things
be printed so that His Highness might read them with greater ease. And
that is the purpose of the following Epitome, or account, most highly
abbreviated.

Presentation by Bishop don Fray Bartolomé de las Casas
or Casaus, to the most high and potent lord Prince
of all the Spains don Felipe, our lord

Most high and potent lord:

Because divine providence has ordered in this world that for the direc-
tion[7] and common utility of the human lineage the world be constituted by Kingdoms and peoples, with their kings like fathers and
shepherds (as Homer has called them) and therefore the most noble
and generous members of the republics, for that reason no doubt of the
rectitude of the royal spirits of those kings may be held, or with right reason might be held. And if any wrongs, failings, defects, or evils should
be suffered in those kingdoms, the only reason for that is that the kings
have no notice of them. For these wrongs &c, if they be present and reported, it is the duty of the king, with greatest study and vigilant indus-
try, to root them out. This appears to have been the meaning of divine
scripture in the proverbs of Solomon: *Rex qui sedet in solio iudicii, dissi-
pat omne malum intuito suo.*[8] For it is clear that with the innate and natural virtue of the king, the mere notice of wrong or malefaction in his

---

[6] Prince Philip, later King Philip II, was at that time in charge of matters relating
to the Indies. Only son and successor to Emperor Charles V and Isabel of Portugal, Philip
married four times—to Maria of Portugal (1543), to Mary Tudor of England (1554), to
Elizabeth of Valois in France (1560), and to Anna, daughter of Emperor Maximilian II
(1570).

[7] Guidance.

[8] "A king that sitteth in the throne of judgment scattereth away all evil with his
eyes" (Proverbs 20:8).

kingdom more than suffices for him to scatter it, and should such ills arise, not for a single moment could he tolerate them.

Considering, then, most potent lord, the evils and harm, the perditions and ruin—the equals or likes of which, never were men imagined capable of doing—considering, as I say, those evils which as a man of fifty years' and more experience, being in those lands present, I have seen committed upon those so many and such great kingdoms, or better said, that entire vast and new world of the Indies—lands conceded and given in trust by God and His Church to the king and queen of Castile, to rule and govern them, convert them to belief in Christ and the Holy Catholic Church, and give them to prosper temporally and spiritually—, this subject was not able to contain himself from supplicating with Your Majesty, most importunely, that Your Majesty not concede such licence nor allow those terrible things that the tyrants did invent, pursue, and have committed against those peaceable, humble, and meek Indian peoples, who offend no person. For these are things that are iniquitous, tyrannous, and condemned, detested, and accursed by all natural, divine, and human law (though they be called "conquests"), yet which, if they be allowed, those evil men shall, most surely, commit once more. Considering, then, the perditions of infinite souls and bodies that those subjects had once perpetrated and would again, I, not being a prisoner rendered mute, deliberated to put into writing, so that Your Highness might more easily read them, some—a very few—examples that in days past I had collected from among the countless number that I could in truth declare.

And as the archbishop of Toledo, teacher of Your Highness, was bishop of Cartagena, he did ask that account of me and presented it to Your Highness, but because of the long paths of sea and land that Your Highness has traveled, and the frequent royal occupations Your Highness has had, it may be that either Your Highness did not read that account or has forgotten that Your Highness has it. And yet such is the temerity and unreasonable[9] eagerness of those who think nothing of spilling such immense quantities of human blood and depopulating those vast lands of their natural inhabitants and possessors, killing a thousand million souls and stealing incomparable treasures, that it grows stronger every day, and so by divers paths and several feigned colours these tyrannical men importune that they be conceded or allowed said conquests (which cannot be conceded to them without violation of natural and divine law, and therefore commission of most grave

---

[9] Irrational, mad.

mortal sins, worthy of terrible, eternal torments). Thus I thought it right to serve Your Highness with this brief and abbreviated summary of that otherwise voluminous narration of the devastations and perditions which might be, and ought to be, composed. I beg that Your Highness read it with the generosity and royal benignity that is Your Highness' wont with the works of those subjects and servants of thine who desire to serve purely and solely to further the public weal and the prosperity of the royal estate. And once Your Highness has seen the deformity of the injustice which upon those innocent peoples is done, destroying them and cutting them to pieces without cause or just reason for it, but rather out of mere covetousness and ambition of those who pretend to do such nefarious deeds—once this deformity has been seen, I say, and has been understood, I beg that Your Highness be kind enough to supplicate and persuade His Majesty[10] to deny any man who might propose to undertake such noxious and detestable enterprises, and instead lay perpetual silence upon that infernal request, with such fear and terror that no man might thereafter dare even so much as name it.

This is a thing, my most high lord, which is most sorely needful and necessary so that God might make the entire estate of the royal crown of Castile prosper spiritually and temporally, and preserve it and bestow upon it blessings. Amen.

[An Introduction to the Relation]

The islands of the Indies were discovered in the year 1492. They began to be inhabited[11] by Christian Spaniards in the year following, and thus it has been but forty-nine years[12] since Spaniards in great numbers went forth to those Islands. And the first land into which they entered for the purpose of inhabitation was the large and well-favoured Island of Hispaniola, which is six hundred leagues[13] in compass. There are infinite

---

[10] The Emperor Charles V.

[11] Populated, settled.

[12] *Brevísima Relación* in this form was completed in 1542, though there is a kind of afterword appended that was written in 1547, and then an imprimatur that indicates a printing date of 1552.

[13] This is not the standard English league, but a unit of measure used in the 15th and 16th centuries in Spain. (For all terms relating to weights, measures, and political or administrative entities, see the Table of Weights and Measures, p. 121, and following.) Here and throughout, Las Casas' distances are estimates—speculative at best, and generally exaggerated by a figure of two or more. In this case, the figure given is about double the true circumference of Hispaniola.

other exceedingly large islands lying everywhere about this Hispaniola, and all of them were, and were seen by us to be, as populous and filled with native-born peoples, the Indians, as any peopled land upon the earth. Terra Firma, which lies at its nearest point two hundred fifty leagues distant, or some few more, possesses a sea-coast of above ten thousand leagues discovered (and more is discovered every day), all filled as though the land were a beehive of people, at least so far as to the year 1541 has been discovered. And so it would appear that God did set down upon those lands the entire multitude, or greatest part, of the entire human lineage.

All these universal and infinite peoples *a toto genere*,[14] God created to be a simple people, altogether without subtility, malice, or duplicity, excellent in obedience, most loyal to their native lords and to the Christians whom they serve; the most humble, most patient, meekest and most pacific, slowest to take offence and most tranquil in demeanor, least quarrelous, least querulous, most lacking in rancour or hatreds or desire for vengeance of all the peoples of the earth. They are, likewise, the most delicate, slender, and tender of complexion[15] and the least able to withstand hard labour, and are those who most easily die of any sort of illness or disease, for not even the children of princes and lords among us, raised with gifts and in delicate living, are more delicate than these native Indians, even those born to the lineage of labourers and those who till the fields. They are also the most impoverished of nations, those who possess and desire to possess the fewest temporal goods, and thus they are never proud, never ambitious, never covetous. Their food is such that the food of the holy fathers in the desert would seem not to have been more austere or frugal or less delightful. Their dress is generally nakedness itself, with naught but their private parts covered, or at the most, a kind of cotton shawl, which I estimate to be between a *vara* and a half and two *varas* of cloth on each side. They make their beds upon a piece of mat, or at the farthest they may sleep upon a thing they contrive which I might liken to a fishing-net drawn together at each extreme and therefrom suspended, which in the language of the island of Hispaniola they call *hamacas*.[16]

These people are among the cleanliest and most unoccupied of the inhabitants of the earth, and of a lively understanding, very apt and

---

[14] Of all kinds.

[15] Physical constitution.

[16] *Hamaca* (hammock) was one of the Caribbean Indian (Taino) words that found its way into several European languages; "hurricane" and its cognates, for example, is another.

tractable for all fair doctrine, excellently fit to receive our holy Catholic faith and to be indued with virtuous customs, and the people with the fewest impediments to this that God has created upon the earth. And from the moment they begin to learn about the elements of the faith, they are so importunate to know it, and to enter in the sacraments of the Church and holy worship, that I say truth when I declare that the priests and friars must be graced with the most singular degree of patience in order to bear them. And finally, I have been told by many other Spaniards who have been in that place for many years (those not of the cloth, I mean to say), and many times I have heard them say it, that the goodness they see in these Indians is not to be denied: "In sooth, these peoples were the most fortunate in the world, if they but knew God."

Into and among these gentle sheep, endowed by their Maker and Creator with all the qualities aforesaid, did creep the Spaniards, who no sooner had knowledge of these people than they became like fierce wolves and tigers and lions who have gone many days without food or nourishment. And no other thing have they done for forty years until this day,[17] and still today see fit to do, but dismember, slay, perturb, afflict, torment, and destroy the Indians by all manner of cruelty—new and divers and most singular manners such as never before seen or read or heard of —some few of which shall be recounted below, and they do this to such a degree that on the Island of Hispaniola, of the above three million souls that we once saw, today there be no more than two hundred of those native peoples remaining. The Island of Cuba is almost as long as from Valladolid to Rome; today it is almost devoid of population. The Island of San Juan[18] and that of Jamaica, large and well-favoured and lovely islands both, have been laid waste. On the Isles of the Lucayos[19]—which lie next the Islands of Cuba and Hispaniola on the north and of which there are above sixty that are called the Giants and other islands both large and small, the least-favoured of them being more fertile and lovely than the garden of the king in Seville, and the

---

[17] I.e., since 1502, the year Las Casas first went out to the Indies with the expedition led by Nicolás de Ovando. Las Casas is, then, implying that his *Brevísima Relación* will be based on personal experience and observation. It should be noted that Las Casas did not adopt the views expressed in this account until 1514, twelve full years after he came to the Indies. He was, in fact, an *encomendero* at first, one of those who exploited the Indians, and it was not until he was exposed to the ideas of Antonio de Montesinos, a Dominican who preached that the Indians were "men," with souls, that Las Casas' eyes were opened to the brutality of the Conquest.

[18] I.e., Puerto Rico.

[19] The Bahamas.

most healthful land upon the earth—where there were once above five hundred thousand souls, today there is not a living creature. All were killed while being brought, and because of being brought, to the Island of Hispaniola when the Spaniards saw that their stock of the natives of that latter island had come to an end. Indeed, a ship sailing among those islands for three years, seeking to find the people who once lived there, after they had been plucked off (for a good Christian man was moved by pity for those who might be found, to convert them and win them over to Christ) found but eleven persons, which number I saw myself. Another thirty islands which lie about the region of the Island of San Juan are for the same reason desert and unhabited. It would seem that all these islands, the land part of them extending for above two thousand leagues, are unhabited and despoiled of people.

As to the great Terra Firma, we are certain that our Spaniards, through their cruelties and vile acts, have laid those lands waste and depopulated them, and they are today desert and unhabited, though once filled with reasonable[20] men, above ten kingdoms of them, larger than all of Spain, though Aragon and Portugal included, and more land than there be from Sevilla to Jerusalem twice over, which is above two thousand leagues.

We hold as a thing most certain and true that in these forty years there have been above twelve million souls—men, women, and children—killed, tyrannically and unjustly, on account of the tyrannical actions and infernal works of Christians; and in truth I do believe, without thinking to deceive myself, that they were above fifteen million.

Two principal and general customs have been employed by those, calling themselves Christians, who have passed this way, in extirpating and striking from the face of the earth those suffering nations. The first being unjust, cruel, bloody, and tyrannical warfare. The other—after having slain all those who might yearn toward or suspire after or think of freedom, or consider escaping from the torments that they are made to suffer, by which I mean all the native-born lords and adult males, for it is the Spaniards' custom in their wars to allow only young boys and females to live—being to oppress them with the hardest, harshest, and most heinous bondage to which men or beasts might ever be bound into. To these two forms of infernal tyranny, as though to genuses,[21] may

---

[20] Rational, endowed with reason; not today's sense of "sensible, having sound judgment."

[21] A simile from logic, not biology; the concept of biological genuses still lay in the future.

be reduced or subsumed or made subordinate all the other divers and several ways, which indeed are infinite, of laying waste to those peoples.

The cause for which the Christians have slain and destroyed so many and such infinite numbers of souls, has been simply to get, as their ultimate end, the Indians' gold of them, and to stuff themselves with riches in a very few days, and to raise themselves to high estates—without proportion to their birth or breeding, it should be noted—owing to the insatiable greed and ambition that they have had, which has been greater than any the world has ever seen before. For those lands were so favoured and so rich, and the people thereupon so humble, so patient, and so easy to subject, yet the Christians have had no more respect for them, nor have had for them no more account or estimation (I speak truly, for I know and have seen the entire time) than—I would not say for beasts, for pray God that being beasts, the Christians might have respected them and treated them with some gentleness and esteem—but less than the dungheaps of the towns. And so it is in that wise that they have seen fit to cure their souls and their bodies, wherefore all the numbers and millions aforesaid have died without the faith and without the sacraments of the church. And it is a very well known and well attested fact, which all persons, however tyrannous and murderous they may be, do know and confess: That all the Indians of all the Indies never once did aught hurt or wrong to Christians, but rather held them to be descended from heaven, from the sky, until many times they or their neighbours first received from the Christians many acts of wrongful harm, theft, murder, violence, and vexation.

On the Island Hispaniola

On the island Hispaniola, which was the first, as we said, wherein the Christians entered and began the devastations and perditions of these nations, and first destroyed them and wiped the land clean of inhabitants, these Christians began to take the women and children of the Indians to serve them and use them ill, and they would eat their victuals that issued from the sweat of their brow and their hard work, and yet still were not content with what the Indians gave them willingly, according to the ability that each one had, which is not ever much, for they seldom have more than that which they have most immediate need of and can produce with little labour. And in truth, what suffices for three houses of ten persons each for a month, a Christian will eat and destroy in one day, and these Christians did them many other acts of compulsion and violence and vexation.

The Indians, at this treatment, began to see that those men must not have come down from the sky, or heaven, and some hid their victuals, others their women and children, while others fled into the wilderness to remove themselves from men of such hard and terrible conversation.[22] The Christians would smite them with their hands and strike them with their fists and beat them with sticks and cudgels, until they finally laid hands upon the lords of the villages. And this practice came to such great temerity and shamelessness and ignominy that a Christian captain did violate the wife of the greatest king, the lord of all the island.[23] And at that, the Indians began to seek ways to cast the Christians from their lands; they took up arms, which are but weak and petty things, of little offence and resistance and even less defence (for which reason, all their wars are little more than what would be games with wooden swords here in this land, or even children's games), and at that, the Christians with their horses and swords and pikes and lances began to wreak slaughters and singular cruelties upon them.

They would enter into the villages and spare not children, or old people, or pregnant women, or women with suckling babes, but would open the woman's belly and hack the babe to pieces, as though they were butchering lambs shut up in their pen. They would lay wagers who might slice open the belly of a man with one stroke of their blade, or cut off a man's head with one swift motion of their pike, or spill out his entrails. They would snatch babes from their mothers' breasts and take them by their feet and dash their heads against the rocks. Others would fling them over their shoulders into the rivers, laughing and jeering, and as they fell into the water they would call out: "Thrash, you little bugger!"; other babes, they would run their swords through mother and child at once, and all that they came across. They would erect long gibbets, but no higher than that a man's feet might dangle just above the ground, and bind thirteen of the Indians at one time, in honour and reverence, they said, of Our Redeemer and the twelve Apostles, and put firewood around it and burn the Indians alive. Others, they would tie or bind their bodies all about with dry straw, and set fire to the straw and burn them that way. Others, and all those that they desired to let live, they would cut off both their hands but leave them hanging by the skin,

---

[22] I.e., social intercourse, treatment of others.

[23] Las Casas is referring to the case of the Spanish *encomendero* Francisco de Valenzuela, who raped the wife of the cacique Enriquillo. Enriquillo had been raised in the Franciscan monastery at Vera Paz, and he was in constant revolt against the Spaniards between 1519 and 1538, when Charles V ordered that a peace treaty be signed with him—the first such treaty in the New World.

and they would say to them: "Go, and take these letters," which was to say, carry the news to the people who have hidden themselves in the mountains and the wilderness. They would often slay the lords and nobles in this way: They would weave together twigs and branches, like unto a gridiron, but made of twigs, and raise it on forked poles or limbs of trees set into the ground, and tether the lords and nobles to that grate and set a slow fire below it, so that little by little, crying out and screaming from those torments, and in desperation, they would give up their souls.

I myself saw that once, four or five lords and men of high rank were being burned on grates in this way (and I even think that there may have been two or three pairs of grates on which others were also being burned), and on account of their loud cries and clamours, the captain seemed to take pity on them, or perhaps they disturbed his sleep, and he ordered them hanged; but the executioner that was burning them, who was worse than any hangman (and I know what his name is and even met certain kinsmen of his in Seville), was not content to hang them, and so with his hands he sewed their mouths shut with sticks, so that

They would erect long gibbets . . . and bind thirteen of the Indians at one time, in honour and reverence, they said, of Our Redeemer and the twelve Apostles, and put firewood around it and burn the Indians alive.

They would weave together twigs and branches, like unto a gridiron . . . and tether the lords and nobles to that grate and set a slow fire below it, so that little by little, crying out and screaming from those torments, and in desperation, they would give up their souls.

they could make no sounds, and then poked up the fire and roasted them as long as he had first desired. I vouchsafe that I did see all the things I have writ above, and infinite numbers of others. And because all those who were able to flee, did hide themselves in the wilderness and go up into the mountains to escape those men who were so inhumane,[24] so pitiless, and so savage, and such abominable destroyers and foremost enemies of the human lineage, the Spaniards taught and trained hunting hounds, fierce and savage dogs that would no sooner see an Indian than they would tear him to pieces, and would rather set upon a man and eat him than if he were a pig. These dogs wrought dreadful havoc and butcheries. And because sometimes, though seldom, the Indians would slay a Christian, though for good and just reason and in holy justice, the Spaniards made a law amongst themselves

---

[24] Sixteenth-century spelling for "inhuman," but still having the modern sense "lacking in all human qualities, feelings, etc." or "destitute of natural kindness, pity, etc."

that for every one Christian that the Indians slew, the Christians would slay an hundred Indians.

On the Kingdoms That Once Were to Be Found upon the Island of Hispaniola

On this island of Hispaniola there were five principal kingdoms of great extent, and five most powerful and mighty kings, whom the other lords, countless numbers of them, all obeyed—or almost all, for there were lords who ruled over some very distant provinces who recognized no man whatsoever over them. One kingdom was called Maguá, with the last syllable accented, which means "the kingdom of the fertile lowland plain."[25] And this plain is one of the most illustrious and remarkable things in the world, for it extends for eighty leagues from the Southern Sea to the Northern.[26] It is five leagues wide, and sometimes eight and even ten, and has highlands in one part and another. It is crossed by above thirty thousand rivers and streams, among them twelve as large as the Ebro and Duero and Guadalquivir;[27] and all of the rivers that flow down from a mountain which is to the west, which number twenty and twenty-five thousand, are most extraordinarily rich in gold. In that mountain, or mountain range, lies the province of Cibao, from which comes down that gold high in carats which is so famed here. The king and lord of this kingdom was called Guarionex, and his vassals were such great lords that one of them might bring together sixteen thousand fighting men to serve that greater lord, and I met some of them. This king Guarionex was very obedient and virtuous, and naturally peaceable and devoted to the king and queen of Castile; and in certain years his people, upon his command—each person who had a house—gave the hollow of a gourd filled with gold, and then afterward, unable to fill them to the top, they would cut the gourd in the middle and fill that half and give it, because the Indians of that island had very little or no skill for taking the gold from the mines. This cacique[28] would offer to serve the king of Castile by tilling land that extended from Isabela,

---

[25] In Spanish, "la vega"; La Vega is now the place-name of a city just south of Santiago, Dominican Republic.

[26] From the Caribbean on the south to the Atlantic on the north.

[27] The largest rivers in Spain.

[28] "*Cacique*" is the Caribbean native peoples' word for their chief or ruler (feminine, *cacica*), and because Las Casas uses it with such familiarity and frequency it will not

which was the first town made by the Christians, to the city of Santo Domingo, which is fifty leagues or more, if they would not ask for gold, because he would say, and soothfully, that his vassals did not know how to get it. The farming that he said he would do, I know he was able to do it, and would do it with great pleasure, and I also know that it would be worth more to the king each year than three million *castellanos*, and so rich and fertile was the land on which he would farm that it would give sustenance for above fifty cities as large as Sevilla, were it used in that wise today.

The coin in which they repaid this good high king and lord was to dishonour him with his wife, an evil Christian captain being the man who violated her. And the lord, to buy time and bring together his people to take vengeance, resolved to flee and hide himself, alone, and if need be to die in exile from his land and estate within a province that was called the land of the Ciguayos, where lived a great lord his vassal. And when the Christians found him gone, they would not have it that he be kept from them; they went and made war on the lord who had him, where they committed great slaughters, until at last they found him and seized him, and bound him in chains and shackles, and put him into a boat to bring him to Castile. Which boat was lost at sea, and with him were drowned many Christians and a great quantity of gold, among which perished the great lump that was as large as a loaf of bread and of weight three thousand six hundred castellanos. And God did in this wise wreak His vengeance for such great injustices.

The other kingdom was called the kingdom of Marién, where Puerto Real is now, at the extreme of the plain toward the north, and larger than the kingdom of Portugal, although in truth much more rich and fertile and apt for inhabitation,[29] and containing many large mountains and rich mines of gold and copper, and its king was called Guacanagarí, with accent upon the last syllable, under whom there were many very great lords, of whom I saw and met many. And it was upon the land of Guacanagarí that the former Admiral[30] who discovered the Indies first

---

be italicized or otherwise indicated as "foreign" in these pages. In fact, the Spaniards adopted "cacique" as their word for native chief all over the Americas, and it has come to be used commonly today to mean "political boss" both in Latin America and in Spain.

[29] The reader is reminded that this means "fertile and apt for *settlement*," not simply "for living"; Las Casas is thinking of adding to Spain's wealth by true colonization rather than through mere exploitation, through agriculture as well as with hard metal.

[30] Columbus, in late 1493; and "former" distinguishes Christopher from his son Diego, who succeeded him to the title. In his reports, Christopher Columbus notes his "friendship" with a king whom he does not name but who, as is clear both from Las Casas and other chroniclers and letter-writers, is indeed Guacanagarí.

stopped, and it was this Guacanagarí who received the Admiral the first time, when he discovered the island, and he met him with such humanity and courtesy, and all the Christians that were with him, and made them such a gentle and courteous welcome and aid and provisioning (the Admiral's ship having been lost just there), that in his own land and by his own parents the Admiral could not have been received better. And this I know from the Letter and the words of the Admiral himself. And yet this king died fleeing from the Christians' slaughters and cruelties, destroyed and stripped of his estate, wandering in the wilderness. All the other lords, his subjects, died under the tyranny and in the servitude that shall hereafter be recounted.

The third kingdom and realm was called Maguana, a land likewise admirable, healthful, and fertile, where now the most excellent sugar of the island is made. The king of this kingdom was called Caonabó, and in vigour and state and gravity, and ceremonies in his service, he exceeded all the others. He was taken[31] with great subtility and guile, while he lay, suspecting nothing, in his house. He was afterward put into a ship, to bring him to Castile, and as six ships were in port, waiting to set sail, God manifested His will against that great iniquity and injustice and many others, and sent that night a storm which sank all the ships and drowned all the Christians who were in them, and therein died Caonabó as well, laden down with chains and shackles. This lord had three or four brothers, equally as manly and vigourous as himself; and seeing the unjust capture and imprisonment of their brother and lord, and the destructions and slaughters that the Christians were then committing in the other kingdoms, they took up arms, especially from the moment that they learned that the king their brother was dead, to go and attack and have vengeance upon the Christians. The Christians went against them with a number of horse[32] (which is the most pernicious weapon that there may be among the Indians) and wrought such devastation and slaughter that they laid waste and depopulated half of all that kingdom.

The fourth kingdom was called Xaraguá. This was like the kernel or marrow, or the court of all that island; in its highly polished tongue and speech, in the courtesy and most orderly and composed breeding[33] of its people, in the number of its nobility and their generosity—because

---

[31] Seized, captured.

[32] Cavalry, horsemen, of course, although in the parenthesis that follows, it is the animal *horse* that is the fearsome weapon because of its speed.

[33] Manners; cf. "a person of good breeding," implying courtesy and mannerliness.

there were many, a great number, of lords and nobles, and in the prettiness and beauty of all the people, it exceeded all the others. The king and lord of this kingdom was called Behechio; he had a sister who was called Anacaona. This brother and sister did great services to the king and queen of Castile and immense benefices to the Christians, freeing them from many perils of imminent death; and after king Behechio had died, his sister the lady Anacaona remained as queen. And to this kingdom there came one day the governor[34] who ruled this island, with sixty horse[35] and three hundred foot[36] or more, though those on horse be enough to lay waste to the entire island and Terra Firma. And above three hundred lords and nobles went out to him when he called them, promising them no harm, and he commanded that most of those lords be put by deceit and guile into a very large house of straw, and when they were closed up within, he ordered that the house be set a-fire and those lords and nobles be burned alive. And then they rushed upon all the others and put an infinite number of people to the sword, and the lady Anacaona, to show her the honour due her, they hanged her. And it came into some Christians' minds, either out of pity or because of greed, to take some children to raise them and not kill them, and so they put them up behind their horses, but another Spaniard came up and ran them through with his lance. Another, seeing a child lying on the ground, cut off its legs with his sword. Some of those who were able to flee this inhumane cruelty went over to a small island that is some eight leagues over the sea from there, and that same governor sentenced all those that had fled there to be made slaves, because they had fled the slaughter.

The fifth kingdom is called Higüey, and over it there was an old queen who was called Higuanama. This lady was hanged, and infinite was the number of people that I saw burned alive and hacked to pieces and tortured by divers and new ways of killing and torment, and all those taken alive were made slaves. And because there have been so many particular cases of slaughter and perdition of those people and those nations that even long recounting would not suffice to tell them (for in truth I do believe that however much is told, not a thousandth part may be explained, nor much less understood), I will conclude by saying and declaring with respect to those wars aforesaid, that by God and my conscience I am certain that for the Spaniards to commit all the

[34] Nicolás de Ovando.
[35] Cavalrymen.
[36] Foot soldiers, or infantrymen.

acts of injustice and evil that I have told, and the others that might be told, the Indians gave them no more cause nor were any more to be blamed for it than a monastery of good honest monks might give a man for robbing them or slaying them, and those monks who escaped the slaughters alive, putting them in perpetual bondage and servitude as slaves. And I would say further, that until at last all the many people and nations of that island had been slain and laid waste they did not commit against the Christians, so far as I can believe or conjecture, a single mortal sin punishable by man. And those sins which are reserved for punishment by God alone, such as a desire for vengeance, or the hatred and rancour that those peoples might harbor against such capital enemies as the Christians were to them, into these I believe very few Indians ever fell, and they were little more impetuous and hard, by the great experience that I have of them, than children of ten or twelve years old. And I know, too, as a sure and infallible truth, that the Indians always waged the most just and defensible war against the Christians, albeit the Christians never waged just war against the Indians, but rather were diabolical and infinitely unjust, and much more so in that wise than might be held or said about any tyrant in the world at any time before. And the same I do declare about all the wars that have been fought in all the Indies.

After these wars had ended, and all the men slain in them, so that there were generally left only young boys and women and children, the Spaniards parcelled them out amongst themselves, giving one thirty, another forty, another an hundred and two hundred (depending upon the grace which each one had curried with the tyrant-major, whom they called governor). And when the Indians were distributed among each Christian, the Spaniards coloured what they had done in the following way: That they would teach the Indians the things of the Catholic faith, although generally these were men who were idiots and cruel, exceedingly avaricious and filled with vice, though they set themselves as curates and priests of souls. And the care that they gave these souls was to send the men into the mines to dig out gold, which is intolerable work, and the women they set to work on their *estancias*, which are farms, to dig in the fields and till the land, which is labour not for women but for strong, robust men. They would give neither the men nor the women any food to eat, but rather grass and things of no solid substance. The milk dried up in all the mothers who were suckling their babes, and soon all the newborn babes died. And since the husbands were far off, and never saw their wives, procreation ceased among them. The men died in the mines from hard labour and starvation, and the women on the farms for the same cause, and so multitudes of men and women and children of that island died, and so all the people of the earth might have died as well. If a man were to tell the burthens they put upon them, which were three and four *arrobas*, and to be carried for an hundred and two hundred leagues,[37] and the Christians even had themselves borne in *hamacas*, which are like fishing-nets, on the backs of the Indians, because they always used them like beasts of burden (the Indians would have galls and sores on their shoulders and backs, from the burthens they were made to carry, like ill-used beasts), and to tell how they would whip, buffet, cudgel, and smite them, strike them with their fists, curse them, and inflict upon them a thousand other kinds of torture and torment while they were at work, then in truth within a little time there would be no paper that could bear such telling, and no man that could bear the horror.

And I pray that it be noted here as well, that the perdition of these islands and lands began to increase from the time the news came of the death of her most serene highness the Queen Doña Isabel, which was the year 1504, because until then some provinces only had been destroyed on this island by unjust wars, but not all of them, and these destructions, most of them or almost all, were kept from the knowledge of the queen. Because the queen, may she dwell in Glory, took exceedingly great care and admirable zeal for the salvation and prosperity of those peoples and those nations, as those of us know who saw and touched with our own eyes and our own hands examples of this.

And another rule should be noted in this: That in all the parts of the Indies where Christians have gone and have passed, they always wrought upon the Indians all the cruelties set forth above, and carried out their abominable slaughters and tyrannies and oppressions upon those innocent peoples. And ever would they pile on many more and greater and newer forms of torture, and they would comport themselves ever more cruelly, for God had allowed them to fall ever lower and to hurl themselves ever deeper into accursed judgment.

On the Two Islands of San Juan and Jamaica

The Spaniards passed on to the Island of San Juan and the Island of Jamaica, which were gardens of fruits and foodstuffs and hives of bees and

---

[37] A conscious exaggeration on Las Casas' part; the Dominican report of 1519, on which he bases this claim, states that the native island porters were forced to carry burdens of two *arrobas* (fifty pounds) for distances of sixty to seventy leagues. Thus, Las Casas doubles these figures. In the absence of beasts of burden such as horses, human portage was institutionalized throughout the pre-Columbian Americas.

honey, in the year 1509, for the same purpose and end with which they had entered into Hispaniola.[38] And they committed the great offences and sins set forth above, and added many more singular and terrible cruelties besides, slaying and burning the Indians and laying them upon those aforesaid gridirons made of twigs and tree branches to roast them and setting loose savage dogs, and afterward oppressing and torturing and ill-treating them in the mines and other labours, until they had consumed and worn away all those poor innocents and slain them. On those two aforesaid islands there had once been above six hundred thousand souls, and I believe above a million, and yet today there are no more than two hundred persons on each, all having perished without faith and without sacraments.

On the Island of Cuba

In the year 1511, the Spaniards passed on to the island of Cuba,[39] which, as I have said, is as long as from Valladolid to Rome (and where there were once great provinces of people), and they began and ended in the manners spoken of above and many more, and more cruelly. Here there occurred most singular and abominable things.

There was a high cacique and lord, whose name was Hatuey, who had gone from the island of Hispaniola to Cuba with many of his people, fleeing the calamities and inhumane deeds of the Christians, and being at that time on that island of Cuba, and wishing to give certain news to the Indians there that the Christians would be coming on to that island, he gathered together many or all of his people, and he spoke to them thus: "You know that it is said that the Christians are soon to be coming here, and you have experience of what has happened to lords

---

[38] Las Casas is referring to the expeditions of Juan Ponce de León (1460–1521) and Juan de Esquivel (d. 1513) to Puerto Rico and Jamaica, respectively. The city of Ponce in Puerto Rico was named in honor of Ponce de León, who later claimed and explored Florida and the island of Bimini in the Bahamas that he considered to be the fountain of eternal youth. Esquivel, a native of Seville, founded Salvaleón de Higüey in Hispaniola between 1502 and 1506. After his conquest of Jamaica he founded several towns. To the great disappointment of his sponsors, King Ferdinand and Governor Diego Columbus, he found no gold in Jamaica. A bauxite and aluminum loading port on the south coast of Jamaica bears his name.

[39] Las Casas is referring to the expedition of Diego Velásquez y Cuellar (1465–1524), the governor of Cuba, under whose auspices Hernán Cortés sailed to Mexico in 1519.

so-and-so and so-and-so and so-and-so; and how those Christians have used[40] those nations of Haití (which is Hispaniola), and they are now coming here. And do you know perchance why they do this?" And they replied: "No, save that they are by their nature cruel and evil." And he says: "They do it not for that reason alone, but rather because they have a god that they worship and love much, and to make us love him they work to subjugate us and slay us."

He had a small basket nigh beside him, filled with gold and gems, and he said: "You see here the god of the Christians: let us do, if you think it right, *areytos* (which are their dances) to him, and perhaps we can please him and he shall command them not to do us harm." And all the Indians there shouted out to him: "That is good, that is good." And they danced before him until they had all wearied, and afterward the lord Hatuey said: "Look, even so, if we keep him, to get him from us they shall surely slay us; let us throw him into this river." And all vowed to do that, and so they threw the basket into the river, a large river that was thereby.[41]

This cacique and lord was constantly fleeing from the Christians, from the moment they came to that island of Cuba, being one who knew them well, and he would defend himself when he came upon them, but at last they captured him. And for no reason but that he fled such iniquitous and cruel people, and defended himself from those who wished to slay him and oppress him until the death of him and all his people and the succeeding generations, they burned him alive. And when he was bound to the stake, a friar of the order of Saint Francis, a holy father who was thereby, spoke some things to him concerning God and our faith, which he had never heard before—or as much as what that friar was able in the short time that the executioners gave him— and the friar asked if the lord wished to believe those things that he told him, for if he did he would go to the sky (that is, heaven), where there was glory and eternal rest, but if not, he would certainly go to hell and suffer perpetual torments and sufferings. And thinking a while, the lord asked the holy father whether Christians went to the sky. The priest replied that they did, but only those who were good. And the cacique then said without thinking on it any more, that he did not desire to go to the sky, but rather down to hell, so that he would not be where *they* were and would not see such cruel people. And this is the fame and

---

[40] Treated.

[41] This was probably the Toa River, which flows near Baracoa in northeastern Cuba.

honour that God and our faith have won by the work of those Christians who have gone out to the Indies.

Once, some Indians were coming out to us to receive us with victuals and gifts ten leagues from a great village, and when we came to them we were given a great quantity of fish and bread and food and all else that they were able. But suddenly the devil came upon the Christians, and in my presence they took out their knives (with no reason or cause that might be alleged in justification) and slew above three thousand souls who were sitting there before us, men and women and children. And there I saw such great cruelties that no living man had never seen the like of them before, or thought to see.

Another time, a few days thence, I sent messengers to all the lords of the province of La Habana, assuring them not to fear (for they had heard of me to my credit), telling them not to absent themselves but to come out to receive us, that no harm whatsoever would be done them (for the entire land was stricken with horror at the slaughters that had

[T]he lord asked the holy father whether Christians went to the sky. The priest replied that they did, but only those who were good. And the cacique then said . . . that he did not desire to go to the sky, but rather down to hell, so that he would not be where they were and would not see such cruel people.

been done), and this I did with the consent of the captain. And when we arrived at the province, they did come out to receive us, some twenty-one lords and caciques, and afterward the captain, in breach of the assurances that I had given them, took hold of them and desired the next day to burn them alive, saying that it was right, because those lords must at some time have committed some act to merit it. And it was most difficult for me to save them from the pyre, but at last they did escape it.

After all the Indians of this island were cast into the same servitude and calamity as those of Hispaniola, seeing all of themselves and their people die and perish without any help for it, some began to flee into the wilderness, others to hang themselves in desperation and lack of hope, and husbands and wives to hang themselves together, and with them, hang their children. And because of the cruelties of one most tyrannous Spaniard (whom I met), above two hundred Indians hanged themselves. An infinite number died in this manner.

There was an officer of the king upon this island who was given as *repartimiento* three hundred Indians, and at the end of three months two hundred and sixty of them had died in the labours of the mines, so that no more than thirty remained, which was the tenth part of them. After that, he was given as many more again, or more even than that, and he also slew these, and he would be given more, and slay more, until at last he died and the devil had his soul.

In the three or four months that I abode there, above seven thousand children starved to death, because their fathers and mothers had been carried off to the mines. And many other such heinous things of that kind did I see.

After that, they resolved to go out and search for the Indians who had fled into the wilderness and the mountains, and there they wrought terrible havoc and devastation, and so thoroughly laid waste to all that island and left it unhabited, as we ourselves saw not long ago, that it is a great shame and pity to see it bare and waste and rendered a very desert of solitude.

On Terra Firma

In the year 1514 a wretched governor came to Terra Firma,[42] a most exceedingly harsh and cruel tyrant, of no pity nor even prudence, like

---

[42] Las Casas is referring to Pedro Arias Dávila (1440?–1531?), often written Pedrarías Dávila or de Avila, a Sevillan conquistador of Jewish ancestry who fought in Africa

unto an instrument of divine wrath, very much on purpose to inhabit that land with many Spaniard men. And although divers tyrants had gone to Terra Firma and robbed and slain and left many people outraged, it had been along the sea-coast, raiding and pillaging what they could. But this one exceeded all the others who had gone before him, and those of all the islands, and his most execrable and evil deeds exceeded all the abominations of the past; and he did not depopulate and slay only along the sea-coast, but also in great lands and kingdoms, casting great numbers of peoples and entire nations that lived within them into the fires of hell.[43] He slew the inhabitants from many leagues above Darién to the kingdom and provinces of Nicaragua, and Nicaragua itself with them, which is above five hundred leagues, and the best and most fertile and populous land that it is believed ever to have been seen upon the earth, where there were many great lords, infinite numbers of large settlements, and exceedingly great treasures of gold. Indeed, until that time in no place had there appeared upon the surface of the ground so much gold, because Spain had been filled almost to overflowing with the gold of Hispaniola, of finer quality, but it had been taken by the Indians out of the entrails of the earth, from those mines that we have spoken of, where, as we have said, they died.

This governor and his people invented yet new manners of cruelties and of giving torments to the Indians, so that those poor wretches would reveal and give them gold. There was one of his captains who in an attack he made (at the other's command) to rob and murder people, slew over forty thousand souls, which was seen with his own eyes by a priest of the order of Saint Francis who went with him, called Fray Francisco de San Román. In this, the captain put them to the sword, burned them alive, set savage dogs upon them, and tortured them with divers tortures.

And the most exceedingly pernicious blindness that those who have ruled the Indies have always had, down even to this very day, with respect to disposing and ordering the conversion and salvation of those peoples—a thing which they have always put off for another day (and this I say in truth) both in work and in effect, though in their words they have always pretended and coloured and feigned otherwise—this blind-

---

and was named governor of Darién in 1514 to replace Vasco Núñez de Balboa, whom Arias Dávila beheaded in 1519. Arias Dávila founded Panama in 1519 and set in motion the pacification of Nicaragua, which was under way when he died in 1531.

[43] Always in Las Casas' mind is the Catholic doctrine that teaches that those who are not brought into the Catholic faith and Church must inevitably, when they die, be sent to hell; so here there is no implication that the Indians have acted badly or that these governor-tyrants have the power of ecclesiastical condemnation.

ness, as I say, has reached such a degree that they have imagined[44] and practiced and commanded that the Indians be read a *requerimiento*,[45] requiring that they come into the faith and render obedience to the king and queen of Castile, and telling them that if they do not do this, then fiery, bloody war will be waged upon them and they will be slain and captured, &c. And this is as though the Son of God, who died for each of them, had commanded in His law, when he said *Euntes docete omnes gentes*,[46] that a demand be read to peaceable and quiet unbelievers who are in possession of their own lands, and if they heeded and obeyed it not, though having no other preaching or doctrine, and gave themselves not over to the governance of a king that they had never heard of nor seen, especially one whose people and messengers were so cruel, so harsh and pitiless, and such abominable tyrants, then they would forfeit their chattel and their lands, their liberty, their women and children and all their lives, which is a thing that is absurd and foolish and worthy of all vituperation and derision and of hellfire. Yet since that wretched and accursed governor carried orders instructing that the aforesaid *requerimientos* be given, in order to justify them yet more (their being in themselves absurd, unreasonable, and most exceedingly unjust), he commanded, or the thieves and robbers that he sent did so, when they resolved to go a-raiding and robbing in some village of which they heard that it had gold, that the wretched raiding Spaniards go in the night to within half a league of the village, while the Indians were in their villages and in their houses fearing no harm, and there, that night, they should read out the *requerimiento* to themselves, saying: "Caciques and Indians of this Terra Firma of such-and-such a village, we do hereby give you notice that there is a God and a pope, and a king of Castile who is the lord of these lands. Come then to give him obedience, &c. For if you do not, know ye that we shall wage war upon you, and shall slay you and capture you, &c." And at the fourth watch,[47] while the innocent Indians were sleeping with their women and children, they would rush upon the village, putting fire to the houses, which generally were of straw, and burning the children and women and many of the others alive, before they knew what was upon them. They would slay

[44] I.e., devised, plotted.

[45] This new law or royal edict was put into effect in 1513, and the text given by Las Casas substantially reproduces the text of the *requerimiento* ("demand" or "charge") that was to be read to any native peoples "discovered" or come upon by the Spaniard explorers/conquistadors/settlers.

[46] "Go ye therefore, and teach all nations" (Matthew 28:19).

[47] That is, just at dawn or shortly before.

any they desired, and those whom they took alive they would torture them to death, in order that they might tell them of other villages with gold, or more gold than was found there, and those who remained they would put them in irons as slaves. And they would then go, when the fire had abated, to search out the gold that there might be in the houses. And this man lost to perdition occupied himself in this wise and in these deeds, with all the evil Christians that he took with him, from the year 1514 until the year 1521 or 1522, sending on those raids five and six and more underlings, for which they would give him as his portion so many parts (in addition to that which was his right as captain-general) of all the gold and pearls and gems that they stole and the slaves they made. And in this same wise did act the officers of the king, each one sending as many servants or underlings as he could, and the highest and foremost bishop of that kingdom would also send those who served him so as to have his part in that harvest. More gold did they steal in that time from that kingdom (as I can judge) than one million *castellanos*, and I do believe that I fall short there, yet it will be found that they sent not to the king but three thousand *castellanos* of all they stole. And more men and women and children did they destroy than eight hundred thousand souls. The other tyrannical governors who succeeded[48] there, down to the year 1533, slew and allowed to be slain, in the tyrannical bondage that followed upon the wars, all those who remained.

Among the infinite acts of evil that this man did and allowed to be done in the time in which he ruled was that, a cacique or lord giving him, either of his own will or out of fear (which is more likely true) nine thousand *castellanos*, being not content with this, they laid hold of that lord and tethered him to a stake set in the ground, and extending his feet, they set fire against them so that he would give them more gold. And so he sent to his house and another three thousand *castellanos* were brought. And once again they tortured him, and the lord, not giving more gold (whether because he had no more or because he would not), they held him in this manner until the marrow came out the soles of his feet, and so he died. And like this death, infinite were the times that they slew lords and tortured them to get gold from them.

Another time, as a certain captain of the Spaniards went a-raiding, they came to a wilderness or deep forest in which, fleeing from those so foul and abominable deeds done by the Christians, many people had come together to hide themselves. And the Spaniards rushed suddenly in among them and took seventy or eighty maidens and women and

---

[48] Came after, followed, were his successors.

killed as many male Indians as they were able. The next day a great number of Indians came together and followed after the Christians, to fight to recover the women and children. And when the Christians saw that they were hard set upon, they refused to release their spoils, but rather ran their swords through the bellies of the girls and women, and of the eighty they held captive, left not one alive. The Indians, who were tearing at their skin in grief, were crying out and saying: "Oh, evil men, cruel Christians, you have killed *iras!*" In that land they call women *iras*, as though saying: Killing women is a sign of abominations and cruel beastly men.

Ten or fifteen leagues from Panamá there was a great lord called París, and very rich in gold. The Christians went there, and he received them as though they were his brothers, and made a gift to the captain of fifty thousand *castellanos* of his own will. The captain and the Christians, it seemed to them that any man who gave that amount of his own courtesy must have a great treasure (which was the end and consolation of all their labours), and so they feigned and said that they wished to depart, but they returned at the fourth watch and set upon the village, and burned it with a fire that they set, slew and burned many people, and stole fifty or sixty thousand *castellanos* more. And the cacique or lord escaped; he was not taken or slain. And soon he gathered all the people that he was able, and in two or three days he overtook the Christians who were carrying away his one hundred thirty or forty thousand *castellanos*, and he slew fifty Christians and took from them all the gold, while the others escaped in flight, gravely wounded. Afterward, many Christians returned to that cacique, and they laid waste to him and infinite numbers of his people, and the others they seized and killed them in base servitude. And so today there is neither trace nor sign that any village ever was, or man born there, where there was once thirty leagues filled with the people of that lord's rule. And of like deeds, countless are the slaughters and perditions that that wretched man did work with his company in those kingdoms.

On the Province of Nicaragua

In the year 1522 or 1523, this tyrant next subjugated the most exceedingly fertile province of Nicaragua, for which his entrance marked a dark hour.[49] Of this province, what man might tell the happiness,

---

[49] Here again Las Casas is referring to Pedro Arias Dávila.

health, amenity, and prosperity and populousness of its people? It was a
thing of wonder, in sooth, to see how filled it was with villages, which
extended for almost three and four leagues in length, filled with admirable groves of fruit trees that caused the people to be immense. And
because it was a land that is flat and without features, so that the people
there could not abscond into the wilderness of forest or up into the
mountains, and delightful, so that they were grieved and in anguish to
think of leaving it, they thus did suffer terrible persecutions and all that
it was possible for them to tolerate of bondage and acts of tyranny at the
hands of the Christians (for by their nature they were a most meek and
pacific people). That tyrant and the tyrannical companions who were
with him, all those who had aided him to destroy that entire other kingdom, did the Indians so much harm, wrought upon them such slaughters, such cruelties, so many captivities and injustices, that no human
tongue can tell it. He would send out fifty men of horse and command
that an entire province, greater than the country of Rusellón,[50] be put to
the lance, and leave not a man or woman or old person or child alive,
for any slightest thing, or because they did not come soon enough to his
summons, or did not carry so many *cargas* of maize, which is the wheat
of those lands, or give up so many Indians to serve him, him or another
of his company; because, since it was flat land, no man might flee the
horses, or their hellish wrath.

He would send Spaniards to make *entradas*, which is to go off to
other provinces to make raids upon the Indians there, and he would
allow the raiders to carry off all the Indians they desired from their
peaceable villages, to serve them, and they would put them in chains so
that they would not leave behind the burthens weighing three *arrobas*
that he set upon their backs. And it fell out one time, of the many times
that he did this, that of four thousand Indians, not six returned alive to
their houses, for he left them all dead upon the roads. For when some
would grow tired and their feet be tired and bloody from the great burdens and they would sicken from hunger and hard labour and weakness, so as not to unshackle them from the chains he would cut off their
heads at the neck, and the head would fall to one side and the body to
the other. Conceive what the others would have felt. And so, when the
Spaniards would order such processions, the Indians having the experi-

---

[50] In modern Spanish, *Rosellón*, known in English/French as *Roussillon*, the former name of a province or county on the Mediterranean in southern France, now called
Pyrenées-Orientales, bordering Spain on the north (i.e., above Barcelona and Gerona);
this region was part of the kingdom of Aragon, but was ceded to France in 1659 by the
Treaty of the Pyrenees.

ence that none would ever return, as they were departing they would weep and sigh, saying: "Those are the roads which we once took to go and serve the Christians, and although we laboured hard, we would return after some time to our homes and our women and our children, but now we go without hope of ever again returning or seeing them or even being alive."

Once, because he would[51] make a new *repartimiento* of Indians, for so it came into his mind and he would not be denied (and they even say that it was to rid himself of the Indians of his that he did not like and give them to those that he desired to), he was the cause that the Indians did not plant a crop that year, and since there was no food for the Christians, they took from the Indians all the maize they had put by to nourish themselves and their children, and in this wise above twenty or thirty thousand souls did die, and there were women who slew their own children to eat them, so great was their hunger.

Since the villages that they had were all, and each one, a most gracious garden, the Christians took up residence within them, each one in the village that had been his *repartimiento* or (as they call it) his *encomienda*, and tilled the land in them, maintaining themselves upon the poor and meagre victuals of the Indians. And so they took for themselves the Indians' lands that they had and that they had inherited, and which nourished them. And the Spaniards had all the Indians—lords, old persons, women, and children—within their own houses, and they would have them serve them night and day, without respite or rest, and even the children, as soon as they could walk, were occupied in doing all they could, or even more. And so they have consumed them, and still this day consume the few who still remain, without allowing them to have their own house or any possession, in which treatment they exceed all the injustices of this kind that are done even in Hispaniola.

They have wearied and oppressed and been the cause of the rapid death of many people in this province, by making them carry wood and planks from thirty leagues away to the harbour to make boats with, and sending them to find honey and wax into the forests and the wilderness, where they are eaten by tigers.[52] And they have heavily and grievously weighed down, and still do weigh down in this wise today, pregnant and suckling women like beasts of burden.

---

[51] Wished, intended; here, stubbornly insisted on.

[52] Any of the large cats of Central and South America (jaguar, etc.); the Spaniards had not yet adopted the native peoples' names for these cats and so gave them the name they brought from Europe.

The most heinous and detestable pestilence that has laid waste to that province has been the licence[53] which that governor gave to the Spaniards in demanding slaves of the caciques and lords of the villages. They would make demand every four or five months, or whensoever each one obtained that governor's grace or license, requiring fifty slaves of the cacique, with the threat that if he gave them not, he would be burned alive or thrown to the savage dogs. Since the Indians generally keep not slaves—for a cacique has two at most, or three, or four—the lords would go through the village and take first all the orphans, and then ask those who had two children to give one, and those with three, two, and in this wise the cacique would obtain the number that the tyrant asked of him, with great cries and weeping from the village, for these are the people who it seems most love their children in the world. And since this would be done so many times, from the year 1523 to the year 1533 they laid waste all that kingdom, because in those six or seven years they sent out five or six shiploads in the slave trade, carrying off all those multitudes of Indians to be sold as slaves in Panamá and Perú, where all of them are now dead, because it is a thing proven and experienced thousands of times, that when Indians are taken from their native lands, they more easily die, for the Spaniards always fail to give them food yet nowise relieve them of their labours, since they do not sell them nor others buy them, but they only work them. In this wise they have taken from that province above five hundred thousand souls of Indians made slaves, though being truly as free as I. And from the hellish wars that the Spaniards have waged upon them, and from the abominable captivity in which they are cast, more again have died than another five hundred and six hundred thousand persons until this day, and still today they are being slain. In a space of fourteen years, all of these devastations have been done. And today, in all that province of Nicaragua there are probably not above four or five thousand persons, and even these are slain every day by the hard service both of hard labour and to the Spaniards' persons and the oppression to which they are put, though this land once was, as I said, one of the most populous provinces in the world.

On New Spain, I

In the year 1517 New Spain was discovered, and in that discovery great atrocities were wrought upon the Indians and not a few deaths committed

---

[53] Freedom.

by those who did discover it. In the year 1518, those who call themselves Christians[54] went there to rob and kill, though they said they were going to make habitations. And since that year 1518 until this day, in the year 1542, all the iniquity, all the injustice, all the violence and tyranny that the Christians had done in the Indies before this time has been exceeded and overpassed, for they have utterly lost all fear of God and of the king, and have forgotten even themselves. Because so many and so terrible have been the devastations and cruelties, the slaughters and destructions, the depopulations, acts of theft, violence, and tyranny, and in so many and such great kingdoms of the great Terra Firma, that all the things that we have said before are as naught in comparison with those that were done there. But though we told them all (which are infinite in number, those we do not recount), they do not compare in number or in gravity to those that since that year 1518 have been done and perpetrated until this day and year 1542. And today, on this day[55] of the month of September, the most grave and abominable are still done and committed, proving the rule that we set down above, that since the beginning, the outrages and hellish deeds have but grown worse and greater.

And so, from the moment of their *entrada* into New Spain, which was the eighteenth day of April in that year 1518, until the year 1530, there passed twelve full years, which was the duration of the slaughters and devastations that the Spaniards' bloody hands and swords did work incessantly for almost four hundred and fifty leagues in compass about the city of México and its surroundings, in which there lay four and five great kingdoms, as large and very nigh as fertile as all of Spain. And all these lands were exceedingly populous and as filled with people as Toledo and Sevilla and Valladolid and Zaragoza, along with Barcelona, because there is not now nor has there ever been so great a population in those cities, however populous they were, as God set in all those leagues I have spoken of above, which to make a circuit of them all, one would journey above one thousand eight hundred leagues. And more than four million souls have the Spaniards slain within those twelve years within those four hundred and five hundred leagues, by knife and by lance, and burning them alive, women and children and young persons and old. And this was done so long as those that called themselves conquistadors (as the saying is) lasted, though these were not conquests but rather violent invasions by cruel tyrants, which are condemned not

---

[54] Probably Francisco Hernández de Córdoba, who arrived in Hispaniola in 1511 and explored Cozumel Island and the coastal area of Yucatán.

[55] Las Casas does not specify the exact date.

only by the law of God but eke[56] by all human laws, for they are much worse than those committed by the Turks to destroy the Christian Church. And all this does not count those who have died and are slain every day in that tyrannical bondage, those vexations and daily oppressions that I have spoken of above.

To be particular, there is no possible tongue, nor could there be any human knowledge or skill, able to relate the heinous deeds which in divers and several parts, together at one time in some places, at divers and several times in others, have been done by those public adversaries and most capital enemies of the human lineage within that compass; and in truth, some further deeds, made by circumstances and qualities to be all the more heinous and abominable, could not be told even with great diligence and time and writing. But some things in some places I shall recount below, though with protestation, and a vow that I do not think I shall explain the thousandth part.

On New Spain, II

Among divers other slaughters, this one was done in a large city of above thirty thousand inhabitants, which is called Cholula: All the lords of the land and of that realm, and foremost all the priests with the highest priest of them all, did come out to receive the Christians in procession and with great reverence and respect, and they did carry them in their midst to lodge them in the city and in the lodging-houses of the highest lord or lords of it. And seeing this, the Spaniards resolved among themselves to make a slaughter there, or a punishment (as they call it), in order to cast and sow fear of them and of their ferocity through-out every corner of those lands.[57] For this was always the Spaniards' resolve in all the lands that they have entered, it is well to note: to wreak cruel and most singular slaughter, so that those meek lambs might tremble before them. And so for this purpose they sent first to call out all the lords and nobles of the city and of all the places that were subject to the city, with the principal lord of all. And as the Indians' lords and nobles came and entered to speak with the captain of the Spaniards, they were taken prisoner without anyone hearing, so as not to carry the news. The Spaniards

---

[57] Despite the frequent assertions of Las Casas that he was eyewitness to all he described, he accompanied neither Pedro Arias Dávila nor Hernán Cortés, to whom he is making reference here.

had requested five or six thousand Indians of them, to carry their burthens; all these came soon after and these, they cast into the patio of the houses. To see all these Indians when they load themselves up to bear the burthens of the Spaniards is to have great compassion for them, and pity, for they come naked as the day they were born, with only their privates covered and small netting bags over their shoulder with their meagre meals, and they are all made to squat down, like meekest lambs. And when all were brought together and crowded into the courtyard with other people who were thereabout, armed Spaniards were set at the gates of the courtyard to stand guard, while the rest laid hand to their swords and put all those sheep to the sword and lance, so that not one might escape, but all were most grievously murdered. After two or three days, many Indians rose up, still alive though covered with blood, for they had hidden themselves and taken refuge under the dead (so many were they); they came to the Spaniards, weeping and pleading for mercy, begging the Spaniards not to slay them. But for these poor souls there was no mercy or compassion, either, but rather as they came forward they were hacked to pieces. All the lords, who numbered above an hundred and were tightly bound, the captain commanded that they be burned and then taken out alive and raised on stakes set in the ground. But one lord, and perhaps the principal lord and king of that land, was able to free himself and he gathered another twenty or thirty or forty men and they went into the great temple they had by there, which was like a fortress, which they called *Cue*,[58] and there he defended himself for much of that day. But the Spaniards, from whom no man nor thing may take refuge, but especially these unarmed nations, set fire to the temple and there they burned them, though they cried out: "Oh, bad men! What have we ever done to you? Why would you kill us? Go ye to México, go, where our universal lord Motenzuma will have his vengeance on you." And they say that as the five or six thousand men were being put to death by sword there in the courtyard, the captain of the Spaniards was singing:

> One flame the Roman City now destroyes,
> And shrieks of people made a dismal noyse,
> While *Nero* sung and, moved with delight,
> From *Tarpey* Hill beheld the wofull sight.[59]

---

[58] This is simply the Aztec word for "temple."

[59] These verses are taken from the 1656 translation of Las Casas' *Brevísima Relación* by John Phillips, titled *The Tears of the Indians*; the Spanish original was a song popular at the time.

Another great slaughter did they make in the city of Tepeaca, which was much larger and more populous than the first, wherein they put an infinite number of people to the sword, with great and particular acts of cruelty.

From Cholula they marched toward México, with the great king Motenzuma sending them thousands of presents and lords and people and fiestas on the way, and upon their entrance onto the great causeway[60] of México, which is two leagues long, Motenzuma sent his own brother, accompanied by many great lords and great presents of gold and silver and clothing. And at the entrance to the city, he himself came out in person upon litters of gold, with all his great court, to receive

All the lords, who numbered above an hundred and were tightly bound, the captain commanded that they be burned and then taken out alive and raised on stakes set in the ground.

[60] So called because the road ("way") was built on a "causey," or mound; Las Casas calls it a *puente*, or "bridge." The road into the Mexico City, or Tenochtitlán, was built across the lake that surrounded the city, and so was a wonder to the Spaniards who first saw it.

them, and he accompanied them to the palaces in which he ordered that they be lodged, that same day, as I have been told by some who were there present. But with some feigning, Motenzuma having no idea of treachery, the Spaniards took this great king and set eighty men to guard him, and afterward they put him in irons.

But setting all this aside, in which there might be great, and many, things to tell, I wish to tell of one singular thing that those tyrants did. The captain of the Spaniards going to the harbour to take as his prisoner another certain captain[61] who was coming against him, and leaving another certain captain,[62] I believe with an hundred or some number more men to guard the king Motenzuma, these latter Spaniards resolved to do another thing to increase the fear of them in all that land— a stratagem (as I have said) which they have often used. The Indians and the lords and people of all the city and court of Motenzuma busied themselves in naught but giving pleasure to their captive lord. And among divers other fiestas which they made for him was in the evenings to come together in all the parts and plazas of the city for great dances such as they do and is their wont, and which they call *mitotes*, as in the islands they are called *areitos*. In these celebrations they take out all their finest clothing and treasures, and all the people do take part, for it is the principal manner of their pleasure. And the noblest and most gentlemanly persons and those of most royal blood, according to their ranks, had their dances and fiestas closest to the houses wherein their lord was captive. In the part nearest to the palaces there were above two thousand lords' sons, the very cream of the nobility of all Motenzuma's kingdom. To these young men went the captain of the Spaniards with a crew of his men, and he sent other crews to all the other parts of the city where these fiestas were occurring, feigning that they were going to watch them, and he commanded that at a certain hour they all attack them. And so he went, and when they were drinking and safe-feeling in their dances, they called out: "Santiago, to them!"[63] and they began with their naked swords to rend those naked, delicate bodies and to spill that generous blood, and they left not a man alive; and the others in the other plazas did the same. This was a thing that cast all those kingdoms and nations into astonishment and grief and mourning, and filled them

---

[61] Pánfilo de Narváez.

[62] Pedro de Alvarado.

[63] Santiago, or Saint James, was the patron saint of Spain and the protector of the protocountry during the *Reconquista* (completed in 1492), the reconquest of Spanish land from the Moors who had conquered and occupied it for almost eight centuries. Thus, "Santiago, to them! [*Charge!*]" was the Spaniards' battle cry.

with bitterness and pain; and from this day until the end of the world, or the Spaniards do away with them all, they shall never cease lamenting and singing in their areitos and dances, as in the *romances* (as we call them here[64]), that calamity and loss of the succession[65] of all their nobility, which for so many years past they had treasured and venerated.

This unjust thing, this cruelty without precedent, being seen by the Indians perpetrated upon so many guiltless innocents who had with tolerance suffered the no less unjust imprisonment of their lord (for he himself had commanded that they not attack or wage war upon the Christians), they rose up in arms throughout all the city and rushed upon them, and wounded many Spaniards, who were hard put to make their escape. But the Spaniards put a knife to the breast of the prisoner Motenzuma and ordered that he send out runners and command that the Indians not attack that house, but to be pacified and at peace. Yet the Indians would not obey their lord in that, but rather held a confabulation among themselves and resolved to choose another lord and captain to direct their battles. And because now that other Spanish captain who had gone to the port was returning, victorious, and was bringing with him many more Christians, and was fast approaching, the Spaniards ceased the combat for three or four days, until he entered the city. And as he entered, with an infinite number of people gathered from all the land, the Spaniards and the Indians fought one another in such wise and for so many days, that fearing they would all die, the Spaniards resolved one night to flee the city. When the Indians learned of this, they killed a great number of Christians on the causeways[66] crossing the

---

[64] These were chivalric romances filled with magic and enchantment; they were extraordinarily popular in Spain at this time: "The coming of printing to Spain around 1473 had given an extraordinary vogue to romances of chivalry, and *Amadis of Gaul* (1508), the most famous of them all, was known in affectionate detail by a vast body of Spaniards who, if they could not read themselves, had heard them told or read aloud" (J. H. Elliott, *Imperial Spain, 1469–1716*, London: Penguin, 1963, p. 64). When the Spaniards were entering Mexico City (Tenochtitlán), one of the soldiers in the expedition, Bernal Díaz, was amazed at what he saw, and he could only describe it in terms of the romance: "When we saw all those cities and villages built in the water, and other great towns on dry land, and that straight and level causeway leading to Mexico, we were astounded. These great towns and *cues* and buildings rising from the water, all made of stone, seemed like an enchanted vision from the tale of Amadis. Indeed, some of our soldiers asked whether it was not all a dream" (Díaz, *The Conquest of New Spain*, London: Penguin, 1963, p. 214).

[65] Generations to come, transmission of the (noble) estate or title, etc.

[66] These, again, are the four great causeways that connected Tenochtitlán, the "city of México," built on a lake, with dry land. Many Spaniards were indeed killed as they

lake, in most high and just warfare, for the most exceedingly just causes that they had, as we have said. And that these causes were just, any reasonable, fair man must acknowledge. Then, when the Christians had reformed, occurred the battle for the city in which they wrought devastations upon the admirable and wondrous Indians, slaying an infinite number of people and burning many, and great lords, too, alive.

After the most exceedingly great and abominable tyrannies that these men committed in the city of México and in the cities and much land around (ten and fifteen and twenty leagues from México, in which an infinite number of people were slain), he passed his tyrannical plague and pestilence farther on, and it did spread into and defile and lay waste to the province of Pánuco, which was a wondrous thing, the multitude of people that the province had and the devastations and slaughters that he wrought there. Then in the same wise they destroyed the province of Tututepeque, and after that the province of Ipilcingo, and afterward that of Colima, and each one of these is more land than the kingdom of León or the kingdom of Castile. To recount the devastations and deaths and cruelties that they dealt the Indians in each one of these provinces would doubtless be a thing exceedingly difficult to accomplish, and impossible to tell, and yet more tedious to hear.

It must be noted here that the title under which they made their *entradas* and by which they began to destroy all those innocents and wipe the inhabitants from those lands which with their great and infinite populace should have caused such joy and pleasure to anyone who called himself a true Christian, was to say that they came to make the Indians the subjects of the king of Spain, and to make them to obey him, and if they should not bow their knees and obey them, they were to slay them and make them slaves. And those who did not come smartly[67] to obey such unreasonable and foolish messages, and to give themselves over into the hands of such iniquitous and cruel and beastly men, the Spaniards would call them rebels who rose up against the service of Your Majesty. And so they have written and communicated it to the king our lord; and the blindness of those who ruled the Indies would not allow them to perceive or understand that which in their law is express, and clearer than any other of its principles, which is: *That no man*

---

made their escape, but many of them were loaded down with gold and other plunder they were trying to take with them, so that many who were not killed by the Aztecs' weapons drowned when they fell off the causeway. The European mythology of the Conquest calls this "the night of sorrows," or *noche triste*.

[67] Quickly, swiftly, sharply.

is or may be called a rebel if he is not first a subject. I pray all Christians
who know something of God and reason, and even of human laws, to
think, how may the news brought so suddenly to any person who lives
upon his land and feels himself safe and secure from harm, and knows
not that he owes anything to any man, and who has his own natural
lords, how may these words stop the heart of any man, when they are
thus suddenly spoke: "Yield thyself up to obey a foreign king, whom
thou hast never seen nor heard, and if thou dost not, be advised that we
shall chop thee into pieces with these swords," especially seeing by experience that they veritably do this terrible thing. And what most in-
spires a man's horror is that those who do indeed render obedience,
they are cast into most exceedingly harsh bondage, where with incredible labour and even more long-extended tortures, in which they last
some time longer than those who are put to the sword, they perish
nonetheless at last, they and their women and children and all their
generation. And when it is under these fears and threats that those peoples, or any other peoples in the world, are at last persuaded to obey and
acknowledge the rule of that foreign king, still those men made blind
and unreasonable by ambition and diabolic greed, those most incon-
stant and accursed *viros*, do not see that that capitulation gives them not
one jot of right. For if it is truly by fears and terrors that those peoples be
subjugated, then according to natural and human and divine law all the
rest that these men do it is naught but air, save it be in atonement for
those sins that shall cast them into the infernal fires, and likewise for the
harm and offence they do the king and queen of Castile in destroying
those monarchs' kingdoms and rendering naught (so far as they are
able) all the right that those monarchs have to all the Indies. And these,
and no others, are the services that the Spaniards have done to that king
and queen in those lands, and still do this day.

  With this most just and approved title, then, that tyrant of a captain
sent another two tyrannical captains, much crueler and more savage
than he, more evil, and with less pity and mercy, to two great and most
flourishing and fertile kingdoms, filled with people and most populous,
that is, the kingdom of Guatimala, which lies upon the Southern
Ocean,[68] and the other Naco y Honduras or Guaimura, which lies
upon the Northern Ocean,[69] bordering one another and both lying at

---

  [68] The Pacific side; Guatemala is the point where Central America rightly begins,
taking a sort of dogleg to the east from the southern border of Mexico. Thus Guatemala,
Honduras, El Salvador, Nicaragua, Costa Rica, and Panama have "northern"
(Caribbean) and "southern" (Pacific) seas.
  [69] The Caribbean.

the terminus some three hundred leagues from México to the south. One he sent by land and the other in ships by sea, each one with many horse and foot soldiers.[70]

I say true that if all that these two men did perpetrate in acts of malice, and most especially he who went to the kingdom of Guatimala, because the other soon found a hard death—if all these malicious and evil acts, I say, all the devastations, all the deaths, all the extirpations of peoples from their lands, all such savage acts of injustice that inspire horror in the centuries present and to come, were expressed and gathered together, they would make a great book indeed, for this captain exceeded all those of the past and present, both in quantity and number of abominations which he did, and in the peoples that he destroyed and lands that he laid waste and made a desert, because the number of all these is infinite.

He who went by sea and in ships wrought great acts of robbery and abuse and violent dispersion of people in the villages along the coast, some of whom came out to receive him with presents in the kingdom of Yucatán, which is on the way to the kingdom I named above, Naco y Guaimura, to which he was bound. After he had arrived there, he sent captains and many men through-out that land, and they robbed and killed and destroyed all the villages and people that were there. And there was one especially who, rising up in mutiny even against his own captain, took three hundred men and pushed inland toward Guatimala, and in this wise he made his way, destroying and burning all the villages that he came upon, and robbing and killing the people who lived in them. And he marched onward in this enterprise above an hundred and twenty leagues, so that if men were sent after him, to capture him, they would find the land laid waste and unhabited, and the Indians thereabout would slay them in revenge for the damage and destruction that the others had left. Within a few days, the Spaniards slew the principal captain who had sent them and against whom this captain had risen in rebellion, and after that there succeeded many other most exceedingly cruel and bloodthirsty tyrants, who—with heinous slaughters and acts of cruelty, and making slaves and selling them to the ships that brought them wine and clothing and other things, and with common tyrannical servitude,[71] from the year 1524 to the year 1535—laid waste to those

---

[70] Las Casas is referring to the expeditions of Pedro de Alvarado (1485?–1541) and Cristóbal de Olid. Alvarado was of that large noble family that sent at least five brothers to Hispaniola by 1510; he saw action in Peru and died in 1541 in Jalisco, Mexico. Not much is known of Olid.

[71] That is, using the Indians as slaves in their personal service, not selling them or otherwise disposing of them.

provinces and the kingdom of Naco y Honduras, which had before
seemed a true paradise of delights and were more populous than the most
frequented and populous land on earth. And now we have passed there
and come that way, and we saw them in such devastation and so wanting
in inhabitants that any person, however hard he might be, his heart would
break with grief to see it. More have died in these eleven years than two
million souls, and within the compass of above an hundred leagues no
more than two thousand people have been left, and of these, more are
being slain every day in that bondage that I have spoken of.

Turning my quill now to speak of the great tyrant of a captain who, as
I have said, exceeded all those in the past and is like unto all those who
live today, he went to the kingdom of Guatimala, from the provinces
bordering México, which by the road he took (as he himself wrote in a
letter to the principal captain who had sent him) is four hundred
leagues distant from the kingdom of Guatimala, and he made his way
committing slaughters and acts of robbery, burning and stealing and destroying wheresoe'er he came, all the land, with that title that I have
spoken of—that is, telling the Indians that they should bow their knees
to them, to these men so inhumane, unjust, and cruel, in the name of
the king of Spain, who is unknown to the Indians and never heard of,
and whom they no doubt deem to be much more unjust and cruel than
his subjects, these unjust and cruel Spaniard conquerors. And without
letting them deliberate upon it one moment, but rather almost as soon
as the message had been read out, they began to kill and burn and
wreak their havoc upon them.

On the Province and Kingdom of Guatimala

When he came to that kingdom, as he made his *entrada* he slaughtered
many people.[72] And despite this, there came out to receive him, upon
litters and with trumpets and tambours and great celebrations, the principal lord with many other lords of the city of Utatlán, the chief city of
the entire kingdom,[73] and they served him with all that they had, especially giving them victuals as was meet,[74] and all that they were able. As

---

[72] Las Casas is referring to the conquests of Pedro de Alvarado in Guatemala in
1524.

[73] Utatlán was the capital of the Quiché kingdom, the largest and politically/
militarily most powerful highland Maya kingdom of the time. The "principal lord" referred to below was Tecum Uman.

[74] Appropriate, fitting, etc.

for the Spaniards, they made a camp outside the city that night, because it appeared to them strong and thus that within, there might be danger. And the day following, he called out the principal lord and many other lords, and when they had come to him like gentle lambs, he laid hold of them all and told them that they were to give him so many cargas of gold. They replied that they had it not, because that land did not bear gold. And so he had them burned alive, with no further guilt or trial or sentence. And when the lords of all those provinces saw that their supreme lord and the other high lords had all been burned, and for no reason but that they would not give them gold, they all fled their villages into the wilderness, and they ordered all their people, that they go to the Spaniards and serve them as if they were their masters, but not reveal where they had gone. All the people of the land came to the Spaniards then and told them that they belonged to them and that they would serve them as their masters. This pious captain replied that he would not receive them, and indeed that he would have them all burned alive unless they revealed where their lords had gone. The Indians said that they knew not, that he was to employ them as he would, them and their wives and children, who could be found in their houses, and there they might slay or do with them as they would, and many times the Indians said this and offered this and did this. And it was a wonder to see, that the Spaniards went to the villages, where the poor people were working at their labours with their wives and children safe by, and there they ran them through with their spears and hacked them into pieces. And to a very great and powerful village they came (its people more careless than others, and thinking in their innocence that they were safe) and the Spaniards entered and in a space of two hours almost razed them to the ground, putting children and women and old persons to the sword and slaying as many as they could, who, though fleeing, did not escape.

And when the Indians saw that even with so much humility and offerings and patience and suffering they still could not break or soften such inhumane and bestial hearts, and that so without appearance or colour of reason, and indeed so perfectly contrary to it, they were hacked to pieces, and seeing that they were to die for no cause and in the very twinkling of an eye, they agreed to meet and to join together and to die in war, taking vengeance as best they could upon such cruel and hellish enemies, for they well knew that being not just unarmed, but naked, on foot, and weak, against people so fierce, on horseback, and so well armed, they could not prevail, but in the end would be destroyed. Then they invented some holes in the middle of the roads, into which the horses would fall and their innards be pierced through with sharp, fire-hardened stakes driven into the bottom of those holes, which had been covered with grass and weeds so that there might appear to be naught there. But only one time or two did horses fall into them, because the Spaniards learned to guard against them. But to take vengeance even for this, the Spaniards made it law that all the Indians of any sex and age that might be taken alive would be thrown into the holes. And thus pregnant and nursing women and children and old persons and any others that they might take, they would throw them into the holes until the pits were filled, the Indians being pierced through by the stakes, which was a sore thing to see, especially the women with their children. All the others, the Spaniards slew them with spears and lances and knives and threw them to savage dogs that tore them to pieces and ate them. And when the Spaniards came upon some lord, upon my honour they would burn him in a raging fire. They went about these inhumane slaughters for near onto seven years, from the year 1524 to the year 1530 or 1531. Judge for yourself, then, how great was the number of people that must have been consumed.

And thus pregnant and nursing women and children and old persons and any others they might take, they would throw them into the holes until the pits were filled, the Indians being pierced through by the stakes, which was a sore thing to see, especially the women with their children.

Of the infinite abominable works carried out by this wretched, ill-destined tyrant and his brothers (for they were his captains and no less wretched and insensible than he, along with the others that aided them), there was one deed that was especially remarkable. This was in the province of Cuzcatlán, where, or near by, is the city of San Salvador now, which is a most blessed land with all the coast of the Southern Sea, which extends for forty and fifty leagues. And in the city of Cuzcatlán, which was the head of the province, the Spaniards were met with the most regal welcome, and some twenty or thirty thousand Indians awaited them, bearing hens and other victuals. And when this tyrant had arrived and received the presents, he ordered that each Spaniard with him take from among that great number of people all the Indians that they would, so that for the days that they were there the Indians might serve them and be charged with bringing them all the things that they might require[75] or need. And each one took an hundred, or fifty, or the number that each one thought might be needful to be well served, and the innocent lambs were divided and portioned out among them and they served with all their strength, and there was no help but that they worship them. And meanwhile this captain bade the lords bring him great quantities of gold, for it was that that they had principally come for. The Indians replied that they would be pleased to give them all the gold they had, and they gathered together a very great number of axes (which they employ as they will) of gilt copper, which appears to be gold because it does have some. He ordered that the touchstone be brought for them, and when he saw that they were copper, he said to the Spaniards: "To the devil with this land; let's be off, for there is no gold; and each one of the Indians you have that serve you, put them in chains and have them in irons to be slaves." And so they did, and they set them in shackles with the king's irons to be slaves, all of them that could be bound, and I saw the son of the principal lord of that city put in irons. This evil deed being seen by the Indians who were released and by the others throughout the land, the Indians began to come together and to arm themselves. The Spaniards wrought great devastation and slaughter among them, and they turned toward Guatimala, where they built a city, that same city that now, in just judgment, has been destroyed by divine justice with three deluges together, one of water and another of earth and another of stones thicker than ten and twenty oxen.

When all the lords and the men able to wage war had died, the Spaniards cast all the rest into that aforesaid hellish servitude, and by

[75] Ask for, request.

requiring slaves as tribute and being given their sons and daughters (because they have no other slaves), and sending ships filled with them to be sold in Perú, and with other slaughters and devastations which without number they carried out, they have destroyed and laid waste a kingdom of one hundred leagues on a side and above, of the happiest and most fertile and most populous that exists upon the earth. And this very tyrant wrote that it was more populous than the kingdom of México, and he said true: he and his brothers and the others have slain above four or five million souls in fifteen or sixteen years, from the year 1524 to the year 1540, and still today do slay and destroy those that remain, and will surely go on in this wise until all the rest are slain.

It was this man's custom that when he was about to make war upon some villages or provinces, he would take with him all he could of the already subject Indians, that they might wage war upon the others, and since he would not feed the ten or even twenty thousand men that he took with him, he gave them leave to eat the Indians that they captured. And thus there was in his camp the most outright and veritable butchery of human flesh, where in his presence children would be slain and

And thus there was . . . the most outright and veritable butchery of human flesh, where in his presence children would be slain and cooked, and a man would be slain for his hands alone and his feet, which were considered to be a delicacy.

cooked, and a man would be slain for his hands alone and his feet, which were considered to be a delicacy. And with these acts of inhumanity, other peoples of other lands hearing of them, they did not know where to flee, for the terror that they felt.

He killed infinite people in the building of ships. He would drive Indians from the Northern Sea to the Southern, 130 leagues, their backs bent under anchors of three and four *quintales*, with the spurs of the anchors biting into the Indians' backs and shoulders. And he sent in this wise a great deal of artillery, too, upon the shoulders of the poor naked creatures, and I saw many of them burthened with artillery staggering along the roads, despairing and exhausted. He would unmarry and steal from the married men their wives and daughters and give them to the sailors and soldiers so as to make them happy and to take them into his armadas. He swelled the ships with Indians, where all would perish of thirst and hunger. And it is true that if all the particulars of his cruelties should be related, they would make a great book that would inspire the world with horror. Two armadas he made, of many ships each one, and with them he scorched, as though by a fire rained down from heaven, all those lands. Oh! How many orphans did he make, how many fathers did he rob of their children, how many men strip of their wives, how many women leave without their husbands: how many acts of adultery and rapine and savagery was he the cause and reason of! How many persons did he deprive of their freedom, how much anguish and how many calamities did so many men and women suffer because of him! How many tears did he cause to be shed,[76] how many sighs sighed, how many moans and lamentations, how much loneliness and solitude in this world and how much damnation in the other did he cause, not just of Indians, which were infinite, but of wretched Christians as well, who in association with him engaged in such great offences, the gravest sins and most execrable abominations! And pray God that upon him mercy has been visited, and that God be content with the bad end that he at last did come to.

Of New Spain and Pánuco and Jalisco

The Spaniards having wrought the great cruelties and slaughters that we have told of, and others that we have refrained from telling, in the

---

[76] It is this passage that inspired the title of one of the earliest translations of Las Casas' relation, *The Tears of the Indians (etc.)*, by one J. P. (John Phillips of London) in 1656.

provinces of New Spain and the province of Pánuco, in the year 1525 there came to the province of Pánuco another insensible and cruel tyrant.[77] This man carried out many cruelties and put many into irons and made a great number of slaves in the aforesaid manner, though all were once free men, and he sent many ships laden with those unfortunates to the islands of Cuba and Hispaniola, where he was able to sell them more advantageously, and at last he destroyed that entire province, and once even gave for a mare eighty Indians, reasonable creatures.

From thence he was appointed to govern the city of México and all of New Spain, with other great tyrants as *oidores* and himself for the president. There, with the others, he committed such great evils, so many sins, so many cruelties, thefts, and abominations that it could not all be believed. And with these acts they put all that great land in such ultimate depopulation that if God had not restrained him through the resistance of the monks of Saint Francis, and then with the provision of a new *Audiencia Real*, which was good, and the friend of every virtue, in two years he would have left New Spain in the condition in which the island of Hispaniola is today. There was one man in the company of this tyrant who, wishing to enclose a large kitchen-plot of his with a wall, brought in eight thousand Indians to work, without paying them aught or giving them aught to eat, so that of a moment they would fall dead of starvation, and he would not even take notice.

When the principal man of this tyrant, who as I said laid waste to all of Pánuco, received those tidings of the coming of the new *Audiencia Real*, he resolved to make his way inland, to discover other lands to tyrannize, and he took by force from the province of México fifteen or twenty thousand men as bearers of burthens for both him and the Spaniards that went with him, and of this number not two hundred ever returned, and he was the cause of them all dying on the journey. When he came to the province of Mechuacam,[78] which is forty leagues from México, a land as happy and fertile and filled with people as México itself, the king and lord of that place came out to meet him, with a procession of infinite other persons, and made him a thousand gifts and obeisances. He later laid hold of this king because he was famed for being rich in gold and silver, and so that the king might give him great treasures the tyrant began to lay upon him the following torments: He

[77] Las Casas is referring to the conquistador Pedro Beltrán Nuño de Guzmán, the relative of Diego de Guzmán, who served in the Audience of Mexico between 1529 and 1530.

[78] Michoacán, now a state in Mexico.

put him in the stocks by the feet and with the body extended and bound
by the hands to a piece of timber, and he held burning coals to his feet,
and a boy with a horsetail reed wetted with oil would from time to time
sprinkle them with oil to roast the flesh the better; on one side was a
cruel man with an iron crossbow pointed at his heart, and on the other,
another such a one, setting on him a terrible raging dog, which in the
space of a Hail Mary would have torn him to pieces; and thus they tormented and tortured him so that he would reveal to them the treasures
that the captain pretended that he had, until, a certain Franciscan priest
having been advised of all this, he took the poor creature from the captain's hands, although from these torments the Indian later died. And in
this wise they tormented and tortured and killed many lords and
caciques in those provinces so that they might give them gold and silver.

A certain tyrant at this time, going more as a visitor of the purses and
possessions of the Indians, to steal them for himself, than of their souls
or persons, found that certain of them had hidden their idols, for the
sorry Spaniards had never shown them another, better god. He held the
lords until they gave him their idols, thinking them to be of gold or silver, for which he cruelly and unjustly punished them. And so that he
might not be disappointed in his purpose, which was to rob and steal, he
obliged the said caciques to ransom[79] the idols from him, and they pur-
chast them of him for all the gold and silver that they could find, in
order to worship them, as was their wont, as their god. These then are
the works they do and the examples that they give, and the honour those
reprobate Spaniards bring to God in the Indies.

This great tyrannical captain went then from the province of
Mechuacam to the province of Jalisco, which was as whole and meet as
a beehive of happy, populous people, for it is among the most fertile and
admirable lands of all the Indies. Indeed, this province possessed one
village whose population extended for almost seven leagues. And as the
tyrant entered into it, the lords and people came out with gifts and joy,
as all the Indians are wont to do, to welcome the newcomers. And he
began to deal out the cruelties and evil deeds that were his custom, and
that all they had as their custom, and many more besides, in order to
obtain the end that they held as a very god, which is to acquire gold.
They would burn down the villages, lay hands on the caciques, torment
and torture them, and do all this to those they took as slaves. He would
carry away infinite numbers bound in chains, nursing mothers so borne
down with the burthens that they carried—the belongings of the evil

[79] Buy back.

Christians—that, unable to carry their babies for the hardness of the labour and the weakness of starvation, they would cast them down on the side of the road, where infinite numbers perished.

One evil Christian, seizing a maiden by force in order to sin with her, the girl's mother began to rebuke him, crying that he should release her, and she struggled with him; he took out a knife or a sword and cut off the mother's hand, and the maiden, because she would not consent to let him have his way with her, he stabbed her to death.

Among many others, this tyrant had put into irons as slaves, most unjustly (as they were free, like all men in those lands are), four thousand five hundred men and women and one-year-old children suckling at their mother's breast, and others two and three and four and five years old, even those coming out to welcome him in peace, and infinite others, likewise, that were never counted.

When he had waged infinite abominable and infernal wars and had carried out other countless slaughters in these lands, he cast that entire land into coarse and pestilential, tyrannical bondage, which has been the intention and the wont of all the Christian tyrants of the Indies against those peoples. And in this, he gave permission to his very overseers and all the others to carry out cruelties and torments such as never heard of before, in order to take from the Indians gold and tributes. One overseer of his killed many Indians by hanging them and burning them alive and tossing them to savage dogs and cutting off hands and feet and heads and tongues, the Indians being all this while at peace, and for no other cause or reason but to dispirit them and cause them to fear him so that they would serve him and give him gold or tributes, for they saw him and knew him to be a most excellent tyrant, over and above the great many cruel lashes and rods and smitings and other types of cruelty that were done upon them every day and every hour.

It is said of him that he destroyed eight hundred villages and burned them in that kingdom of Jalisco, which was the cause that out of desperation, and having seen all the others so cruelly and unjustly perish, the Indians thereabout rose up and went off into the wilderness and slew, very rightly and honourably, a number of Spaniards. And afterward, with the injustices and insults done them by other new-come tyrants who passed that way in order to destroy other provinces, many of these Indians joined together, gathering their strength in certain crags and precipices, in which now once again such terrible cruelties have been done that the Spaniards have almost succeeded in depopulating and laying waste to all that great land, and slaying infinite people. And the sorry blind creatures, the Spaniards, allowed by God to come to such reprobate mind, do not see the just cause, and indeed several and

divers causes filled with all justice which the Indians posse
divine, and human law for cutting the Spaniards to piec
had forces and arms, and for casting them from their land..,
their own is a most terribly unjust cause, filled with all iniquity and evn,
and condemned by all law everywhere, and that they should desist from
waging yet further warfare, over and above so many insults and tyrannies and such great and inexpugnable sins that they have committed
upon those poor and defenseless Indians. Instead, these Spaniards do
think and say and write that the victories that they have had over the innocent Indians, to extirpate them utterly, all those victories are given
them by God because their evil wars are just, since they revel and glory
in them and give thanks to God for their tyrannies, like unto those thieving tyrants of whom the prophet Zacharias speaks (Chapter 11) when
he says: *Pasce pecora ocisionis, quae qui occidebant non doleban sed
dicebant, benedictus deus quod divites facti sumus.*[80]

On the Kingdom of Yucatán

In the year 1526, another wretched man[81] was made governor of the
kingdom of Yucatán and sent there, thanks to the lies and falsehoods he
told and offerings he made to the king, as the other tyrants have also
done until now, so that they might be given offices and positions from
which they might rob and steal. This kingdom of Yucatán was filled
with infinite numbers of people, for it is land in great measure healthful
and abundant with food and fruits (even more than the land of México)
and particularly abounding in honey and wax above any other part of
the Indies that has so far been seen. It has nearly three hundred leagues
of the tree they call *boja*[82] around about it. The people of said kingdom
were notable among all those of the Indies, both in prudence and policy
and in their lack of vices and sins more than others, and very fit and
worthy to be brought to the knowledge of the Spaniards' God, and their

---

[80] "Feed the flock of the slaughter; whose possessors slay them, and hold themselves not guilty: and they that sell them say, Blessed be the Lord, for I am rich" (Zach.
11:4–5).

[81] The reference is to Francisco de Montejo (1479–1553), who took part in the
conquest of Cuba, founded Vera Cruz in 1519, and began the long conquest of Yucatan
in 1526 that was continued by his son, also named Francisco (founder of Mérida), until
1545.

[82] Probably sagebrush or a similar large flowering shrub.

land a fit place where there could be made great cities of Spaniards and
they might live in them as though in an earthly paradise, were they worthy of it—but they were not, because of their great covetousness and
greed and insensibility and great sins, as they have been unworthy of the
many other parts that God had shown them in those Indies.

And this tyrant began with three hundred men that he brought with
him to wage cruel wars on those good, innocent people, who were in
their houses without offence to any, where he slew and destroyed infinite people. And because the land has no gold—because if it did have,
to take it from the ground he would have killed them all—yet in order
to make gold of the bodies and souls of those for whom Jesus Christ did
die, he brought together all those he had not slain and made them
slaves, and in the many ships that came to the smell and fame of the
slaves, he sent them off filled with people, and they were sold for wine
and oil and vinegar, and for bacon, and for shirts and other clothing,
and for horses, and for what he and they had need of, according to his
judgement and as he saw fit. He would offer up between fifty and an
hundred maidens, one of more lovely appearance than the next, that
each man might choose one in exchange for an arroba of wine or oil or
vinegar, or for a ham, and the same with a well-disposed boy, between
an hundred and two hundred to be chosen, for another such sum. And
it fell out that he gave a boy who appeared to be the son of a king, for a
cheese, and an hundred persons for a horse. And he continued in this
wise from the year 1526 until the year 1533, which were seven years,
laying waste and depopulating those lands and slaying those people
without mercy, until there came the news of the wealth and riches of
Perú, and at that, the Spanish people that were there with him went
straightway to Perú, and that hell that had existed in Yucatán, it ceased
for some days. But then his ministers returned to do great mischief and
thefts and captivities and great offences in the eyes of God, and still
today they cease not to do them, and so they have all those three hundred leagues which were (as I have said) so full and populous, almost
wiped clean of people.

It would be hard to persuade a person to believe, and harder still to
tell, the particular cases of cruelty that have been committed there; I
shall tell but two or three that come to my mind. When the sorry
Spaniards were journeying about with savage dogs, seeking out the Indians and setting those dogs on them, women and men both, one Indian
woman who was ill, seeing that she would not be able to flee the dogs,
to escape them tearing her to pieces as they did to some others, took up
a rope and tied it to the foot of a child she had, of one year old, and she
hanged him from a beam, but she did not do it before the dogs came,

[O]ne Indian woman who was ill, seeing that she would not be able to flee the dogs, . . . took up a rope and tied it to the foot of a child she had . . . and she hanged him from a beam, but she did not do it before the dogs came, and they tore the child apart.

and they tore the child apart, although before he had died completely he was baptized by a friar.

When the Spaniards were leaving out of that kingdom, one of them told the son of a lord of a certain village or province that the son was to come with him; the boy said that he did not want to leave his land. To that, the Spaniard replied: "Come with me, or I shall cut off thine ears." And still the boy said no. And as the boy was saying that he did not wish to leave his land, the Spaniard cut off his nose, laughing as though it were no more than pulling his hair.

This iniquitous man boasted and made much of himself in the presence of a venerable man of the cloth, most shamelessly saying that he worked as hard as ever he was able, to get many Indian women with child so that selling them into slavery pregnant, he might receive that much greater price for them.

In this kingdom, or in a province of the New Spain, a certain Spaniard was going along one day with his dogs to hunt for deer or rabbits, and not finding game, he bethought himself that his dogs were hungry, and he took a little boy from its mother and taking a knife he hacked off its arms and legs, giving each dog its part, and after those pieces had been eaten, he threw the little body onto the ground in among the pack. See, then, how great is the inhumanity and unfeeling-ness of the Spaniards in those lands, and how God has brought them *in reprobus sensus*,[83] and in what esteem they hold those poor people, born and raised up in the image of God and redeemed by His blood. But worse things yet, shall we see below.

Leaving the infinite and never before heard-of cruelties that were done in this kingdom by those who call themselves Christians, and which there is not sufficient mind or reason to think about them, I wish to conclude with only this. Once all the hellish tyrants of this kingdom had left, filled as they were with such eagerness and avidity for the gold and riches of Perú that it fair[84] blinded them, the padre Friar Jacobo[85] set off with four other men of the cloth of his order of Saint Francis to go to that kingdom to pacify and preach and take Jesus Christ to the leav-ings that remained of that hellish harvest and those tyrannical slaugh-ters that the Spaniards had for seven years perpetrated. I believe that those religious fathers went in the year 1534, sending ahead certain In-dians of the province of México as messengers, to ask the peoples they encountered if they would allow said religious fathers to enter into their lands to take them news of our one God, who was the true God and Lord of all the world. And so they entered into council and held many meetings, taking first a great deal of information, what men these were

---

[83] "Of reprobate sense or mind," from Romans 1:28: "And even as they did not like to retain God in their knowledge, God gave them over to a reprobate mind, to do those things which are not convenient." Las Casas has used this phrase twice before, in Spanish, but here he quotes it in Latin, an indication of its Biblical origin. As a member of first the lay orders and then the priesthood, Las Casas always quotes the Bible in Latin, as was the custom in the Catholic Church of the time. Although there had been both "full" and par-tial translations of the Bible (either from Latin and Hebrew or from Greek) into Spanish for some time (as early as the 13th century), those Spanish-language Bibles had been used generally among Jews and *conversos*, especially in the 15th century, or in monasteries among the less well-educated members of the lay orders and the clergy. With the institu-tion of the Inquisition in Spain, however, in the late 15th century, coincident with the ex-pulsion of the Moors and the forced conversion or expulsion of the Jews, combined with the later threat of Protestantism (Luther nailed his famous *Ninety-Five Theses* to the door of the church in Wittenberg in 1517), vernacular Bibles became extremely suspect, and further translation of the Bible into Spanish was halted—indeed prohibited—so that the only Spanish-language texts that could be safely used by readers of the Bible in Spain were glosses and other study aids.

[84] Completely.

[85] Friar Jacobo de Testera was a friend of Las Casas.

who called themselves friars and priests and what it was that they sought and desired, and in what particulars they differed from the Christians from whom they had received so many offences and so much violence and injustice. Finally they agreed to receive them, so long as they only, and no Spaniards, should enter there. The holy fathers made that promise to them, for thus they had been promised in turn by the viceroy of New Spain,[86] who had vowed to them that they might promise that no more Spaniards would enter there, but only men of the cloth, nor that any violence or offence would be done the Indians there by any Christians. They preached to them the evangel of Christ, as is their wont, and the holy intention of the king and queen of Spain toward them. And how much love and savour did the Indians take with the doctrine and example of the friars, and how much pleasure from the news of the king and queen of Castile (of whom in all the seven years past the Spaniards had never spoken, never saying that there was another ruler besides that one who was tyrannizing over them and destroying)! And at the end of forty days since the friars had entered those lands and begun preaching, the lords of the land brought them and delivered up to them their idols, that they should be burned, and after this they delivered up their sons that they should be taught, whom they love more greatly than the light of their eyes, and they made churches and temples for the friars, and houses, and they were invited by other provinces, to go and preach to them and give them news of God and of him who they said was the great king of Castile. And persuaded by the friars, the Indians did a thing that never before in the Indies had been done before, or to this day has been done again, and all those things that are bruited by some of the tyrants who have destroyed those kingdoms and great lands are falsehoods and lies. Twelve or fifteen lords, possessors of many vassals and lands, each one gathering together his peoples and taking their vows and consent, subjected themselves of their own will to the rule of the monarchs of Castile, taking the emperor, as the king of Spain, for their supreme and universal lord, and they made certain signs to affix as though it were their name, which I have in my power as witness of said friars.

And while the friars were yet rejoicing in this progress of the faith, and with the greatest joy and hope of bringing to Jesus Christ all those peoples of that kingdom who from the deaths and unjust wars of the past still remained alive, for there were not a few, eighteen tyrannical

---

[86] Antonio de Mendoza (1490–1552) was viceroy of New Spain between 1535 and 1549. He introduced the printing press and was generally considerate to the Indians, although he refused to fully implement the New Laws in his jurisdiction in 1543.

Spanish cavalrymen, with twelve foot, which were thirty altogether, came into a certain place there, and they brought with them a great load of idols taken from other provinces of the Indians, and the captain of those thirty Spaniards called a lord of this land into which they had entered and told him to take that load of idols and distribute it throughout his land, selling each idol for a male or female Indian to be a slave, and threatening him that if he did not do this, there would be war. This lord, obliged by fear to do what he had been required, distributed the idols throughout his land, and he ordered his vassals to take them and worship them, and to give him male and female Indians to give to the Spaniards to make slaves of them. The Indians, in fear, whoever had two children would give one, and who had three gave two, and in this wise did perform that vile sacrilegious commerce, and the lord or cacique contented the Spaniards, who called themselves Christians.

One of these impious infernal thieves, called Juan García, being taken sick and near to death, had two baskets of idols underneath his bed, and he ordered an Indian woman who served him to see to it that those idols not be given in exchange for chickens or such goods, because they were very good ones, but rather each one for a slave. And finally, with this will and testament, and his mind taken up with this care, the wretch died, and who can doubt that his resting place is now among the fires of hell?

Look now here and consider what the progress and religion and examples of Christianity is of those Spaniards who go to the Indies, what honour they bring to God and procure for Him, in what wise they work so that He may be known and adored by those peoples, what care they take that in those souls there be sown and doth grow and prosper the Holy Faith, and judge whether this sin be less than that of Jeroboam, *qui peccare fecit Israel*[87] by making the two golden calves that the people should worship, or be equal to that of Judas, or more scandal has caused. These, then, are the works of the Spaniards who go to the Indies, which in sooth many, yea infinite times, owing to the greed and covetousness which they have for gold, have sold and still today do sell and deny Jesus Christ, time and time again.

The Indians having seen that it had not been true what the friars had promised them, that no Spaniards should enter, and seeing furthermore that the Spaniards themselves had brought idols from other lands to sell, when they themselves had delivered over to the friars all their own gods

---

[87] "Who made Israel sin," or as the King James version has it, who "drave Israel from following the Lord, and made them sin a great sin" (2 Kings 17:21).

so that they might be burned and one God alone be worshipped, the entire land thereabout rose up in indignation against the friars, and they went to them and said: "Why have you lied to us and deceived us, telling us that no Christians would enter into these lands? And why have you burned our idols, for your Christians bring other gods from other lands, to sell here? Were not our gods better than those of other nations?" The friars appeased them as best they could, though having naught in truth to reply, and they went to seek out the thirty Spaniards, to tell them the harm they had done. They ordered them to go, but they would not, instead giving the Indians to understand that the friars it was who had bade them come to that place, which was a most consummate piece of malice. At last, the Indians resolved to slay the friars; the friars, having been told of the plan by several Indians, did flee one night, and after they had fled, the Indians came to understand the innocence and virtue of the friars and the evil of the Spaniards and they sent messengers for fifty leagues after them, praying that they should turn back and begging their forgiveness for the distress they had caused them. The friars, like the good servants of God that they were, and mindful of those souls, and believing them, returned to that land and were received like angels, the Indians doing them a thousand services, and they remained there for four or five months more. And because those other evil Christians never wanted to depart those lands, nor could the viceroy, despite all his efforts, remove them, for it is far from New Spain (although he caused them to be denounced as traitors), and because they did not cease from working their accustomed insults and outrages upon the Indians, it seemed to the friars that sooner or later, against such evil deeds the Indians would become resentful and perhaps fall upon them. And they thought this especially since they could not preach to the Indians with good conscience about what they would, and without constant alarms owing to the Spaniards' evil works, and so they resolved to forsake that kingdom, and so it was left without the light and sustenance of doctrine, and those souls condemned to that same darkness of ignorance and spiritual poverty in which they then were, for they had been deprived at the most seasonable[88] time of the remedy and watering of the news and knowledge of God, which they had begun to take with the most fervid pleasure, as though we had taken from plants sowed within but a few days, the water of their sustenance. And all this because of the inexplicable sinfulness and consummate evil of those Spaniards.

[88] Favorable, appropriate, "right."

On the Province of Santa Marta

The province of Santa Marta[89] was a land in which the Indians had a very great amount of gold, because the land is rich, and the territories of it, and they had good skill in taking it from the ground. And this was the cause, from the year 1498 until this day, in the year 1542, that no other thing have an infinite number of Spanish tyrants done but go there with ships and raid and rob and slay those people so as to steal from them the gold that they had, and to return in the ships many and many a time, in which enterprise they wrought great havoc and committed untold wanton murders and terrible acts of cruelty, and this generally upon the seacoast and some few leagues more inland, until the year 1523. In that year 1523, Spanish tyrants went there to make an habitation.[90] And because the land, as has been said, was rich, several captains succeeded one another there, some more cruel than others, yet each one seeming to have vowed to work ever more exorbitant cruelties and iniquities upon the Indians than the one before, in order that that rule which we expressed above might be seen indeed to be true. In the year 1529, a great tyrant went there very much on purpose and with many others, with no fear whatever of God or compassion for the race of humankind, which led him to wreak much havoc, many murders and impieties, exceeding, as we have said, all those that had gone before.[91] He and those with him stole many treasures of gold-work in the six or seven years that he lived. After dying without confession, and even fleeing from the residence that he had, there came other murderous and thieving tyrants, who came to put an end even to those who had survived the hands and cruel knife of those tyrants in the past. They spread greatly through the inland lands, laying waste to forests and devastating many and great provinces, slaying and capturing the people of them, employing the

---

[89] On the Caribbean coast of modern-day Colombia.

[90] Las Casas refers here to the many Spanish conquistadors who attempted to establish permanent settlement along that part of the coast, including Alonso de Hojeda, Vasco Nuñez de Balboa (the discoverer of the Pacific Ocean), Alonso de Nicuesa, Francisco Pizarro, and Pedro Arias de Avila, better known as Pedrarías Dávila. This coincides with the eyewitness account of Gonzalo Fernández de Oviedo y Valdés (1478–1557), the official bureaucrat and later chronicler who spent some time in Santo Domingo as well as along the Panamanian coast.

[91] Las Casas is obviously referring to Pedrarías Dávila, but the date is incorrect since Dávila went to Darien in 1517 to take control of the settlements forming along the coast and to contain the aggressive ambitions of Balboa, whom he executed in 1519.

same designs and stratagems as those we have spoken of above, giving great torments to lords and vassals alike, so that they might reveal the gold and the villages that had it. And in their deeds and number and quality, these evil men exceeded, as we have said, all those others who had gone before; and so much exceeded, indeed, that from that year, 1529, until this day, they have depopulated in those parts above four hundred leagues of land which was once as populous as all the others.

I do most truly affirm and vow that if I were to recount, in all their particulars, the evils, slayings, depopulations, injustices, acts of violence, havoc, and great sins that the Spaniards have done in these kingdoms of Santa Marta and committed against God and against the king and those innocent nations, I would make a very long history; but this must await its own time, if God gives life enough. Here I would only say a very few words about those acts concerning which our lord the bishop of that province[92] wrote to the king, and it is the letter of the twentieth day of May of the year 1541, and among other words there are these:

> I say, holy Caesar, that the means to remedy this land is that Your Majesty remove her from the power of her stepfathers and give her a husband who will treat her as reason demands and as she herself merits, and this, in all promptitude; for if Your Majesty does not do this, as these tyrants who have charge of her do weary and afflict her, I am of a certainty that very soon she will cease to be.

And below that it says:

> Wherein Your Majesty will clearly see how those who rule over these parts deserve to be stripped of their ranks so that the republics may have some relief. And if this be not done, it is my belief that their sicknesses shall have no cure. And it is also meet that Your Majesty know that there are no Christians in these parts, but rather demons, that there are no men who serve God or the king, but only traitors to their law and to their king. For it is true that the greatest obstacle that I find, to turning the warring Indians to peace and bringing those at peace into the knowledge of our faith, is the harsh and cruel treatment that the Indians of peace receive from the Christians. Which is the reason that these Indians are so hard of character and so irascible, and naught can be so hateful and odious to them as the name 'Christians,' whom in all this land they call in their tongue *yares*, which is to say 'demons,' and doubtless they are right, for the deeds that are done here are those neither of Christians nor of men who have right reason, but indeed those of demons. And this is the rea-

---

[92] Fray Juan Fernández de Ángulo.

son that since the Indians see how Spaniards act in such evil wise and, generally, so without mercy or pity or fear of God, both in their heads and in their hands, they think that these 'Christians' are but obeying the Christian laws, and that the author of those laws is God and the Christian king. And to attempt to persuade them otherwise is to strain to swallow the ocean itself, and but to give them food for laughter and the where-withal to heap scorn and derision upon Jesus Christ and His law. And since the warring Indians see the treatment that is meted out to those Indians at peace, they believe it better to die once than to die many times in the power and possession of the Spaniards. I know this, invincible Caesar, by experience [&c.].

And further on in that same chapter he writes:

Your Majesty has more servants here than might be thought, because there is no soldier, of all the many that are here, who shrinks from proclaiming publicly that if he assaults or steals, or destroys, or kills, or puts fire to Your Majesty's vassals so that they shall give him gold, he is but serving Your Majesty, for they claim that they have come here upon orders of Your Majesty. And therefore it would be fitting, most Christian Caesar, that Your Majesty have it be understood, by harshly and severely punishing some, that Your Majesty receives no service in a thing that does such disservice to God.

All the above-written are formal words written by the bishop of Santa Marta, and by them one may clearly see what is done today in all those unfortunate lands and against those innocent people. The bishop calls "warring Indians" those who are alive and have been able to save themselves by fleeing into the wilderness to escape the slaughter wrought by the wretched Spaniards. And "Indians at peace" he calls those who, after the death of infinite numbers of their fellows, fall into the abominable and tyrannical bondage described above, where they are finally devastated and slain, as one may see in the words of the bishop; albeit in truth, his words but ill describe what those poor souls are made to suffer.

The Indians in that land say, when they are worn and wearied by bearing burdens through the mountainous sierras, if they fall and grow faint for want of nourishment and from the hard labour (for they are beaten with sticks and cudgels and their teeth are broken with the hafts of swords to make them stand and walk without rest or respite): "Oh, you are evil men. I cannot go on, kill me here, for it is here that I would die." And they say this with great sighing and clutching at their breast, showing great anguish and pain. Oh, who might understand the hundredth part of the afflictions and calamities that those innocent people suffer at the hands of the wretched Spaniards! May God give understanding to those who may and ought to right these wrongs.

On the Province of Cartagena

This province of Cartagena[93] lies fifty leagues under the province of Santa Marta, toward the west, and next it, the province of Cenú, which extends to the Gulf of Urabá, which together have their hundred leagues of sea-coast, and a great deal of land inland toward midday.[94] These provinces, like those of Santa Marta, have been sorely tried, aggrieved, slain, depopulated, and devastated, from the year 1498 until this day, and in them many abominable cruelties have been wrought, and murders and thefts by the Spaniards, which in order to bring a quick end to this brief recount I will not say in particular, and also in order to recount the evil deeds that still today in other lands are done.

On the Coast of Pearls and on
Paria and the Island of Trinidad[95]

From the coast of Paria to the Gulf of Venezuela (exclusive), which is two hundred leagues or thereabouts, great and terrible have been the acts of destruction that the Spaniards have done against those peoples, assaulting them and taking alive as many as they were able, to sell them for slaves. And many times the people are taken in respect of the security and friendship that the Spaniards had forged with them yet thereby keeping neither faith nor truth with them, receiving them in their houses like fathers and children, giving and serving them with all that they had and could.[96] One assuredly could not easily tell or expand in too great particulars what, nor how many, have been the injustices,

---

[93] In Colombia.

[94] I.e., "the south."

[95] Trinidad is an island off the Venezuelan coast, today an independent country (Trinidad and Tobago). Paria is a Venezuelan peninsula that juts out toward Trinidad, which explains Las Casas' phrase that Trinidad is "joined to Terra Firma in the region of Paria."

[96] Here is a case where Las Casas' loose use of "they/them" and his sometimes careless syntax work together to produce a radical ambiguity. It is impossible to tell whether the Spaniards took the Indians into their houses (etc.) or whether the Indians took in the Spaniards, that is, who "they" were and who "them" were. In two earlier translations of Las Casas, one translation reads this sentence one way, the other, the other way. One would assume, of course, from all that Las Casas has said before, that it was the Indians who took in the Spaniards, but it is possible that the Spaniards pretended to offer friendship and hospitality in order to beguile the Indians and lay a trap for them.

insults, wrongs, and outrages that the peoples of this coast have received from the Spaniards, from the year 1510 until this day. I will tell of two or three only, and by them one may judge the other acts, infinite in both number and vileness, which are worthy of all torments, fires, and agonies in the hereafter.

The island of Trinidad, which is much larger than Sicily and more fertile, is joined to Terra Firma in the region of Paria, and the people of that island are of the grandest in spirit and most virtuous of their kind to be found in all the Indies, and in the year 1516 there came to Trinidad a robber and a thief,[97] in the company of another sixty or seventy seasoned brigands, and these men spread the word among the Indians that they had come to make their homes there and live on that island with them. The Indians, both lords and subjects, received them as though they were their dearest children, serving them with the greatest affection and joy, each day bringing them so much food that what remained would serve to feed as many more again. For this liberality is the common custom among all the Indians of that New World: to give even to excess that which the Spaniards need and require,[98] and anything the Indians may possess. They made for the Spaniards a large wooden house in which all of them might live, because that was the Spaniards' wish, one house and no more, in order that they might do what it was their intent to do, and which indeed they did. As the Indians were putting the thatch upon the beams or wood and had covered some two *estados*, so that those who were within could not see those without, the Spaniards, under pretence of making speed to complete the house, ordered many Indians inside it, and they themselves took up posts around it, many of them without the edifice with their weapons, for those who might try to come out, while others were within. And these latter unsheathed their swords and began to threaten the naked Indians, telling them not to move, for if they did they would kill them, and they began to tie them up, while others who leapt up to flee were hacked to pieces with the swords. Some who fled outside, either wounded or whole, and others of the village who had not entered, took up their bows and arrows and gathered in another house in the village to defend themselves; one or two hundred of them entered the house in this wise but, defending the door, the Spaniards set fire to the house and burned them all alive. And with their captives, which numbered some hundred eighty or two hundred men whom they had been able to bind up, they went to their

---

[97] Juan Bono, so specified by Las Casas in his *History of the Indies*, Book III, chapter 91.

[98] Ask for.

ship and raised their sails and sailed to the island of San Juan, where they sold half of them for slaves, and then onward to Hispaniola, where they sold the other half. I reprehended with the captain for this despicable treachery and evil-doing, there on the island of San Juan itself, and he replied: "Forsooth, sir, those were but my orders, for I was instructed by those who sent me, that when I could not take them in war I should take them through peace." And indeed he told me that never in his life had he had a father or mother save on the island of Trinidad, which he measured by the good works that the Indians had done him. This he said to his great confusion, and in insult to his sense. Infinite acts of this sort have been done in that Terra Firma, taking the Indians and capturing them by deceit and treachery. My reader may judge what sort of works these are, and whether those Indians, taken in that wise, whether they have justly been made slaves.

Another time, the friars of Saint Dominic,[99] our order, having resolved to go and preach and convert those peoples who wanted[100] the light of doctrine, to save their souls, which is the state in which the Indies are even today, sent a priest, learned in theology, and of great virtue and sanctity, with a lay brother as his companion, that these two men might see the land and have dealings with the people and find a place apt for making a monastery. These friars having arrived, the Indians received them as though they were angels of heaven and listened with great affection and attention and joy to the words that the friars could make them understand, more by signs than speech, because they did not know the tongue. And it happened that after the ship that had left the friars had departed, another ship passed by there, and the Spaniards on that, without the knowledge of the friars, and by deceit, brought the lord of that land, who was called don Alonso (and either the friars had given him that name, or other Spaniards, because the Indians are very desirous and even greedy to have a Christian name, and they beg to be given one, even before they know sufficient to be baptized), and so they deceived this don Alonso, enticing him to go on to the ship with his wife and certain other persons, telling him that they would make a fiesta for him there. The Indians knew that the friars were in their land and trusted that on their account the Spaniards would not do any evil, because in no other wise would they put their trust in them, and so in the end, seventeen persons went on to the boat with the lord and his wife.

---

[99] Las Casas is referring to the friars Francisco de Córdoba and Juan Garcés. The former died in Cumaná about 1520. Garcés and his ally bishop Zumárraga were considered to be friends of the Indians of New Spain.

[100] Lacked.

And when the Indians had gone on to the ship, the treacherous
Spaniards set their sails and came to the island of Hispaniola, and sold
them for slaves. All the land, seeing their lord and lady carried off, came
to the friars and wanted to slay them. The friars, seeing such great malice done, desired to die of shame and anguish, and one might well believe that they would have given their lives before allowing such a
terrible injustice to be done, most especially because it put a great impediment to their mission, and prevented those souls from ever hearing
or believing the word of God. They conciliated them as best they might,
and told them that with the first ship that passed there they would write
to the island of Hispaniola and require that their lord and all those who
were with him be returned to them.

Some time afterward, God sent a ship to that island, to the greater
confirmation of the damnation of those who ruled, and the friars wrote
to their brethren on Hispaniola. They implored and protested many and
many a time, but the *oidores* would not hear them, and always put aside
their claims for justice, because they had parcelled out among themselves some of the Indians who so unjustly and cruelly had been taken
by the tyrants. The two friars, who had promised the Indians of that land
that their lord don Alonso would return to them within four months,
along with those who were with him, saw that they did not come in four
months, nor in eight, and so they prepared themselves to die and give
their lives for him to whom, before departing, they had offered it. And
so the Indians took just vengeance upon them and slew them, however
innocent they might be, because they believed that the friars had been
the cause of that treachery, and because they saw that it was not true that
within four months, as had been promised and pledged, their lord was
with them again, and because until that time, nor, indeed, until this
day, had they any knowledge, nor do they know even today, that there
was any difference between the friars and the Spanish tyrants and
thieves and robbers and raiders who were a plague upon that land. The
blessed friars suffered unjustly, and by virtue of that injustice there can
be no doubt that in the light of our holy faith they are true martyrs and
sit today at the right hand of God among the blessed, for they came to
that land in an act of willing obedience, and with the purpose of preaching there and spreading the holy faith, and saving all those souls, and
suffering any travail and even death that might be offered them in the
name of our crucified lord and saviour Jesus Christ.

Yet another time,[101] on account of the terrible acts of tyranny and the

---

[101] Specifically during Francisco de Soto's ill-fated attempt at peaceful colonization of Cumaná (January, 1522). See *History of the Indies*, Book III, chapter 159.

despicable works of evil Christians, the Indians slew two other friars of the order of Saint Dominic and one of the order of Saint Francis, of which I am a witness, because I escaped from that same death by a divine miracle, and the telling of it would terrify a man, so great and terrible was the case, but because it would be long to tell, I will save it for its own time. And on the Day of Judgment it shall all be more clear, when God has His vengeance for such heinous and abominable insults as are done in the Indies by those who bear the name of Christians.

Another time in these provinces, in the place they call Cape Codera,[102] there was a village whose lord was called Higueroto, which may be a person's proper name or a name common to the lords of that village. This lord was so good and his people so virtuous that all the Spaniards who came to that place in ships found reparation,[103] food, rest, and all comfort and consolation, and he saved many from death who came starving to him, in flight from other provinces where assaults had been done, and many acts of tyranny and evil-doing. And he restored these Spaniards and sent them whole again to the Island of Pearls, where there was an habitation of Christians, when he could have slain them without anyone being the wiser, but he did not. And at last, all the Christians called that village of Higueroto's *the inn and hostelry of all men.* But soon enough a wretched tyrant resolved to make a raid there, since those people were so secure and unsuspecting. And he went there with his ship, and invited many people to come on to the ship, as they were accustomed to go on to others and to trust in them. When many men and women and children had come on the boat, he raised his sails and came to the island of San Juan, where he sold them all for slaves. And I arrived at that island just then, and I saw this tyrant himself, and I learned there what he had done. He laid waste that entire village, and all the Spanish tyrants who pillaged and assaulted along the coast were grieved by this and execrated this dreadful act, for it caused them to lose the refuge and the hostelry that they had had there, as though they were in their own homes.

I say again that in those lands there have been and still are being done, heinous and horrid acts of malice and evil-doing, and cases to chill the blood, which I omit to tell.

From all that coast, which was once filled with people, they have brought to the island of Hispaniola and that of San Juan two million or

---

[102] About 50 miles east of modern-day Caracas; there now is a town nearby called Higuerote.

[103] In the sense both of "repair," as understood today, and "remedy, especially of the spirit," which is now archaic.

more souls whom they have taken in their raids, and all of those, too, they have slain on those islands and sent to the mines or to other hard labour, over and above the multitudes who lived on them, as we have said above. And it is a great pity and it breaks one's heart to see that coast of fertile, blessed land, now desert and bare of people.

And this is a truth that may easily be confirmed: That they never bring a ship filled with Indians, stolen and assaulted in this manner, as I have said, that they do not cast into the sea, dead, the third part of those who are upon it, having left that many more dead in taking them from their lands. The reason is that, in order to accomplish their ends they must have many people, to obtain more money for more slaves, and they carry but little food or water (so that the tyrants who style themselves "shipowners" may save a little money), hardly enough store, or a little more, for the Spaniards who go in the ship to carry out their raids, and so there is not enough for the poor, sad Indians, and so they die of hunger and thirst, and the answer is to throw them into the sea. And in truth one man who was with them told me that from one island of the Lucayos, where they cause great devastation in this wise, to the Island of Hispaniola, which is sixty or seventy leagues, a ship might sail without compass and without map, taking its course by the trail of Indians floating on the surface of the sea, thrown dead from a ship that went before.

Then, from the moment they remove them from the ship onto the island where they have carried the Indians to be sold as slaves, it would break the heart of any man in whom any jot of mercy were remaining, to see children and old persons, men and women, naked and starving, and falling in a faint from hunger. Then, as though they were lambs, fathers are separated from their sons and wives from their husbands, making herds of ten or twenty persons, and lots are cast for them, so that the groups of them may be carried off by the wretched "shipowners," who are those who put in their part of the money to fit out the armada of two or three ships, and the tyrannical raiders who go out to lay hold of them and set upon them in their homes. And when it happens that within such a lot there is some Indian that is old or sick, the tyrant calls out to the one who is apportioning the lots: "This old man, to the devil with him. What are you giving him to me for, to bury him? This sick one, why should I take him, to cure him?" And one may see here in what great esteem the Spaniards hold the Indians, and may judge whether they obey the divine commandment from which the Law and the Prophets all derive, that men should love one another.

The tyranny that the Spaniards exercise against the Indians in finding or diving for pearls is one of the most cruel and shameful things in the world. There is no hellish and hopeless life on this earth that may be compared with it, however hard and terrible taking out the gold in the mines may be. They throw them into the sea in three and four and five yards' depth from early morning until the sun has set. They are always underwater swimming, without respite, tearing from the seabed the oysters in which the pearls are found. Bearing little nets and gasping for air, they come to the surface, where a Spanish torturer awaits them in a canoe or little rowboat, and if they dally too long in resting, they are beaten and water is poured upon their head to make them dive again. Their food is fish, and also the fish that contains the pearls, and bread made of cassava and sometimes of maize, which are the common breads in those parts, the first of very little substance and the other toilsome to make, and with which they never fill themselves. The beds that they are given of a night is that they are cast into stocks set into the ground, so that they cannot run away. Often they dive into the sea in their fishing or search for pearls and never come up again, because two species of most bloodthirsty and vicious sea beasts,[104] which can swallow a man down whole, do eat them and kill them. And one can see here whether the Spaniards who in their search for pearls act in this wise have obeyed the divine precepts of love for God and man by putting these poor creatures in the way of danger both temporal and of the soul as well, because they die outside the faith and without sacraments, and all for their own infinite greed. And another thing, giving them such a miserable life until they wear them away and consume them in the space of but a few and easily numbered days. Because for men, living under the water without respite is a thing impossible for very long, most especially when the constant coldness of the water penetrates them to their very innards, and so all of them generally die spitting blood from out their mouths, by reason of the tightness of chest that seizes them from being so long and so constantly without respite, and with the diarrhea caused by the cold. Their hair, which is by nature black, becomes burned like the hair of sailors, and salt trails run down their backs, so that they appear to be monsters in the form of men, or another species entirely. In this incomparable labour, or to say the truth, this hellish enterprise, the Spaniards have spent[105] and consumed all the Indians of the Lucayos that once lived on that island when the Spaniards descended into this species of farming. And each one of them was worth fifty or one hundred *castellanos*, and they sold them publicly,

---

[104] Sharks and barracuda, which Las Casas names but for which no words existed in English before the 1580s.

[105] Used up, consumed, worn out.

even though such treatment was forbidden by their own justices (unjust enough, if truth be told), although the Lucayos were fine swimmers. And in these parts there have died countless others from other provinces and parts.

Of the River Yuyapari

Up through the province of Paria there runs a river that is called the River Yuyapari, and it flows above two hundred leagues inland. For many leagues along this waterway there ascended a sorry tyrant in the year 1529 with four hundred men, or some more, and he wrought terrible slaughters, burning alive and putting to the sword an infinite number of innocents who were upon their lands and in their houses and doing no wrong to any man, without care or watch, and he burned a great quantity of land and left it desert and unhabited and as though under a great shadow. And at last he died a terrible death and his armada was portioned out and scattered. And later, other tyrants succeeded him in those malefactions and tyrannies, and still today there are those who pass through those parts, destroying and killing and making a hell for those souls that the Son of God redeemed with His blood.

On the Kingdom of Venezuela

In the year 1526, through deceit and certain malicious persuasions of our lord the king (for men of evil intentions have always worked to conceal from him the harms and perditions that God and the people's souls and the king's estate suffer in those lands of the Indies), the king did give over and concede a great realm, much greater than all of Spain, which is the kingdom of Venezuela, with its entire rule and governance and jurisdiction, to certain merchants of Germany,[106] with a certain capitulation and agreement or assent that he made with them. These men, having made *entrada* into those territories with three hundred men or above, found countless nations as gentle and meek as lambs, like the others (or even more so) who were generally to be found in all parts of the Indies before the Spaniards did them such great harm. These men entered into those lands, then, with more, I do think, incomparable cru-

---

[106] The Welsers, a prominent and powerful banking family.

elty than any of the other tyrants that we have spoken of, and more un-reasonably[107] and furiously than the most bloodthirsty tigers and raven-ing wolves and lions. For with more eagerness and more blind and wrathful avarice, and with much more exquisite skillfulness and inge-nuity in obtaining and robbing silver and gold than all those who went before, and putting aside all fear of God and the king and the shame of humankind, and forgetting that they were mortal men, and with more freedom and brazenness and daring than any others, they took posses-sion of all the jurisdiction of the land.

And these demons incarnate have laid waste, destroyed, and depopu-lated above four hundred leagues of the most fertile lands, and in them grand and admirable provinces, valleys forty leagues in extent, smiling, pleasant regions, large villages filled with a wealth of people and gold. They have murdered and utterly hacked to pieces large and diverse na-tions, devastated many tongues and left no one to speak them, save per-haps some who may have escaped to hide themselves in the caves and innards of the earth, fleeing from this foreign and pestilential knife. And above four and five million souls of those innocent generations (I do be-lieve) they have murdered and destroyed and cast into hell by foreign and divers and new forms of cruel iniquity and impiety; and to this day they have not ceased to cast them, neither. Of the infinite and enor-mous[108] injustices, insults, and devastations that they have committed and do still this day commit, I desire to tell but three or four, by which few cases one may judge what, in order to bring about the great de-structions and depopulations that we have spoken of above, they may have done in all.

They seized the supreme lord of all that province without any cause whatever, to get more gold from him by torturing him. But this lord freed himself and fled, and he went into the wilderness and made a great noise to all the people of that place, and all the people grew so ter-rified that they ran and hid themselves in the forests and wilderness and brambles. The Spaniards made sallies among them in order to go out and find them; and they found them; and they wrought terrible, cruel slaughters, and all those that they took alive they sold them at public auctions for slaves. In many provinces, indeed in all those that they en-tered before they laid hands upon the universal lord, the people would come out to greet and receive them with songs and dances and with many presents of gold in great quantity. The payment that the Spaniards

---

[107] Irrationally, madly, wildly.
[108] Monstrous, shocking.

gave them, though, in order to sow fear throughout that entire land, was to put them to the sword and hack them utterly to pieces. Once, as the Indians came out to receive them in the manner I have described, the German tyrant of a captain ordered a great many people closed up in a house of thatch and hacked to pieces. And since the house had beams up high, many people climbed up into the beams, fleeing the bloody hands of those pitiless men or beasts, and their swords. And so the infernal man ordered that the house be set a-fire, and all those who remained were burned alive. In this wise he stripped many and many villages of every soul, with all the people fleeing for the mountains, where they thought they might find safety.

They arrived in another great province, within the confines of the province and kingdom of Santa Marta. There they found the Indians in their houses, in their villages and haciendas, going about their work and at peace. They sat for a long time with them, eating the fruits of their labours, and the Indians serving them as though they were giving them their very lives and salvation, and also suffering their constant oppressions and ordinary importunities, which are intolerable, for a gluttonous Spaniard eats more in one day than would be sufficient in a month in a house where there are ten Indians. In this time the Indians gave them a great quantity of gold of their own will, with countless other good products that they made them. And after a time, when the tyrants desired finally to go and leave them, they resolved to pay them for their stay in this manner: The German governor, that tyrant (and also, we believe, heretic, for he neither heard mass nor allowed many others to hear it neither, with other signs of Lutheranism that were found out) ordered that all the Indians be taken that could be, with their wives and children, and that they be put in a grand *corral*, or fence made of wooden stakes, that was made for that purpose. And he told them that the man who wished to leave the enclosure and be free had to pay a ransom, to be determined by the iniquitous governor, giving so much gold for himself and so much for his wife and for each child. And to crowd even more Indians inside, he ordered that they not be given any food at all until they had brought forth the gold that he demanded for their ransom. Many sent to their homes for gold and ransomed themselves as they could and they were released and they went home to their labours and to their houses to make a meal. But the tyrant sent certain thieving Spanish raiders who once again seized the poor and already once-ransomed Indians and had them brought to the corral and once again tormented with hunger and thirst until they paid yet another ransom. Of these, there were many who were made prisoners and ransomed two and three times; others, who could not and did not have as much, because they had given all the gold they owned, were left in the *corral* to perish, and they died at last of starvation.

By this act, a province rich in people and in gold, with a valley forty leagues in extent, was left ravaged and laid waste and unhabited, and in that valley also was burned a village that had ten thousand houses.

This hellish tyrant resolved to make his way inland, with cupidity and eagerness to discover in those inland parts the hell of Perú. For this wretched journey he and the others took with them an infinite number of Indians burdened with loads of three or four *arrobas*, and all shackled one to another. Some would grow tired or faint with hunger and hard labour and want of strength, and the tyrant would have their heads cut off at the collar of the shackle so that they would not have to stop to unchain the others that were shackled farther along, and the head would fall to one side and the body to the other, and they would parcel out the dead Indian's load among the loads that the others were carrying. To make an accounting of the provinces that this tyrant devastated, the cities and places that he burned (because all the houses are of thatch), the people that he murdered, the cruelties that in particular acts of slaughter he ordered carried out on this journey, would be a thing that no man might believe, however terrible and true. And along those same ways there came in later times other tyrants who succeeded this one in that same Venezuela, and others in the province of Santa Marta, with the same holy intention of discovering that holy house of gold in Perú, and these latter men found all the land, above two hundred leagues, so burned and depopulated and unhabited, having once been most wonderfully populous and fertile, as we have said, that they, though tyrannical and cruel themselves, marvelled to see the track by which that other cruel German governor had made his way, so waste and lamentable it all was.

All these things are proved, with many witnesses, by the prosecutor for the Council of the Indies, and the proof is in the Council itself, yet they never burned alive any of these vile and execrable tyrants. And what is proved of the great havoc and destruction and evils that those detestable men have done has served for naught, because owing to the great and mortiferous blindness of the ministers of justice who have served in the Indies to this day, none has taken the pains to examine the crimes and perditions and slaughters that have been wrought and are still being wrought by the tyrants of the Indies, save for saying that because so-and-so has perpetrated cruelties upon the Indians, the king has lost of his rents and tributes so many thousand *castellanos*. And to argue this, little proof, and right general and confused proof at that, is sufficient for them. And even this, they know not how to find out or discover, nor what to do, nor how to value it as they ought, for if they did what they owe to God and the king, they would find that these German tyrants have stolen from the king above three million gold *castellanos*. For those provinces of Venezuela, joined with those above four hundred leagues that have most been devastated, laid waste, and depopulated (as I said), is the richest land and the most prosperous in gold, and was likewise in population, that there is in the world. And more rent of them has been obstructed and wasted than the monarchs of Spain received from that kingdom, two million, in the sixteen years since those tyrants who are the enemies of God and the king began to lay them waste. And that loss, from now to the end of the world there is no manner in which it may be recovered, save God miraculously bring back to life so many millions of dead souls. This is the temporal harm done the king of Spain; it would be good to consider what and in what amount is the damage and dishonour, how many the blasphemies, the infamies against God and His law, and with what will be repaid so many countless souls as are now burning in hell because of the greed and inhumanity of those German, or animal, tyrants.[109]

And with only this I would conclude this relation of their wretchedness and ferocity: That since they entered into these lands until today, that is, sixteen years, they have sent many ships loaded and filled with Indians over the sea to be sold for slaves in Santa Marta and on the island of Hispaniola and Jamaica and the island of San Juan. This is above one million Indians, and even today, in the year 1542, they still send them. And the *Audiencia Real* of the island of Hispaniola sees this and dissembles,[110] preferring to favour it like all the other tyrannies and perditions that have been wrought along all that coast of Terra Firma, which is above four hundred leagues that have belonged and still do belong to Venezuela and Santa Marta under their jurisdiction, which they might have halted or against which erected obstacles and remedied. There has been no reason to make all these Indians into slaves save perverse, blind, and stubborn wilfulness, in obedience to the insatiable greed for gold of those exceedingly avaricious tyrants, like all the others in all the Indies have always done, taking and seizing those lambs and sheep from their homes and taking alike their women and children in the cruel and nefarious ways that we have spoken of, and shackling them in the king's irons to sell them for slaves.

---

[109] Here, Las Casas engages in some wordplay in the Spanish, irreproducible in English: *alemán* (German) or *animal* (animal) tyrants.

[110] Pretending not to see or notice.

On the Province of Terra Firma
in the Part Called Florida[111]

To these provinces have gone three tyrants[112] at different times since the year 1510 or 1511, to do the same deeds as others have done, and two of them in other parts of the Indies, so as to raise themselves to states disproportionate to their merits, upon the blood and perdition of their fellow-men. And all three have died most terrible deaths, with the destruction of their persons and the houses that they had built with the blood of men in time past, as I am a witness of all three; and their memory is now wiped from the face of the earth, as though they had not passed through this life. They left the land amazed and aghast[113] and in horror at their name, with some of the slaughters that they committed — and yet truly not so many, for God hath slain them before they could do more, because He had their meet punishment reserved for them, for the evils that I know and saw that in other parts of the Indies they had perpetrated. The fourth tyrant[114] went now at a later time, in the year 1538, very much of a purpose and with great provision. It has been three years now that no one has had knowledge of him; we are sure that after entering those lands he committed cruelties and then disappeared, and if he is still alive, he and his people, in these three years he has destroyed many and grand people if he found them where he travelled, for he is one of those marked out and experienced, and one of those who greatest harm and destruction and evil has done to many provinces and kingdoms, with the other men his companions. But we believe more surely that God has given him the end that He has given other tyrants.

Three or four years after writing what has gone before,[115] there came out of the lands of that Florida we have spoken of, the rest of the tyrants

---

[111] This name referred to virtually all of North America, not just the modern-day peninsula of Florida.

[112] Probably Las Casas has in mind Juan Ponce de León, who died in Havana of wounds received fighting the native peoples of Florida; Pedro de Pineda; and Pánfilo de Narváez (1480–1528), who drowned in the Gulf of Mexico.

[113] Terrified, frightened.

[114] Hernando de Soto (?–1542) ranged widely across the Americas: Darien (1516–1520), Nicaragua (1523), Peru (1531–1536), Florida (1539), and Louisiana, where he crossed the Mississippi in 1540 and died of a fever in 1542 or, according to some accounts, 1543.

[115] Ten years passed between the time Las Casas finished the *Brevísima Relación* (1542) and its publication; this interval left the possibility, here and at one or two other places in the text, for Las Casas to add events that happened or came to light after he had "finished" writing.

who went with that greater tyrant, whom they left dead; and from them
we learned of heinous cruelties and malefactions which mainly he,
when he was alive, and after his wretched death these other inhumane
men did perpetrate there upon those innocent Indians who harmed no
man. And thus we see that that which I had divined above was not in
the end false. And there were so many of those cruelties, that they
proved the rule that we wrote at the beginning above, that the longer
and more thoroughly the Spaniards discovered people and lands and
destroyed them and laid them waste, the more heinous became the cruelties and iniquities against God and their fellow-man that they did perpetrate. But we are wearied by recounting so many and such execrable
and heinous and bloodthirsty deeds, done not by men but by savage
beasts, and therefore I have resolved not to pause here to tell any more
[of those that have come to light], but only the few that follow.

They found great habitations of most well-disposed and intelligent
and politic and well-ordered peoples. And in them, they carried out
great slaughters (as is their wont) in order to fill those people's hearts
with fear of them. They tormented and afflicted them and killed them
by making them fetch and carry like beasts of burden. And when one of
the Indians would tire or grow faint, in order not to remove him from
the shackles and irons to which all the others were bound, in a long
line, they would cut off his head at the neck, and the body would fall to
one side and the head to the other, as we have told in other places.

Entering into a village where they were received with joy and given
so much food that they were soon sated, and above six hundred Indians
to bear their loads and tend their horses, a captain who was a kinsman of
the tyrant-major turned back to sack the entire village, which had
thought itself safe, and he ran the lord and king of the land through
with his lance, and committed other cruelties.

In another large village, as it appeared to them that the villagers did
not come forth so readily as they might, owing to the infamies and
heinous deeds that they had heard told of the Spaniards, they put to the
sword and spear children and adults, babes and old persons, subjects
and lords alike, and showed mercy to none.

A great number of Indians, and especially above two hundred together (as I have heard), which they sent for from a certain village, or
perhaps the Indians came of their own accord, the tyrant-major ordered
his men to cut off all their faces from the nose, with the lips, down to the
chin, leaving them without features. And in this manner, with that pain
and suffering and bitterness, and running streams of blood, they sent
them to carry the news of the deeds and miracles done by those preachers of the Holy Catholic faith, baptized in Jesus' name. And one may

judge in what state those people may be now, how much love they bear for Christians, and what they may believe the God to be whom the Christians hold to be good and just, and the immaculate law and religion that they profess and boast of. Great, passing great and strange are the evil deeds of malice and iniquity that were done there by those wretched men, sons of perdition. And thus, that most wretched captain did die in a state of sinfulness and perdition, without confession, and we cannot doubt but that he is now sunk into the very maw of Hell, save perhaps that God has secretly not sent him there, as His divine mercy and not the worth of the man and his execrable evil-doing, do dictate.

On the Río de la Plata, or the River of Plate[116]

Since the year 1522 or 1523, three or four captains[117] have gone to the River Plate, where there are great kingdoms and provinces and very well-disposed and reasonable people. In general, we know that they have caused deaths and harm; in particular, since it is very remote from that which most touches the Indies, we do not know things in great detail. No doubt have we, however, that they have done, and still are doing, naught but the same deeds that they have done and are still doing in other parts. Because they are the same Spaniards, and among them there are some who have been in the other parts, and because they have resolved and pledged to themselves to become grand and rich lords like the others, yet to be so is impossible save through the perditions and slaughters and thefts and diminution of the Indians, and according to the perverse order and rule and wont that these, like those others, have followed.

After the foregoing was written, we learned how truly we spoke, for they have destroyed and depopulated great provinces and kingdoms of that land, working strange acts of slaughter and cruelty upon those misfortunate creatures, with which deeds they have made themselves remarkable like unto many others, and worse than not a few, for they have had more space in which to work their evil-doing and because they are

---

[116] Silver.

[117] Probably Pedro de Mendoza (1487–1537), who made an attempt to found Buenos Aires in 1536 (the mission gave up, and Mendoza and his group went inland to found Asunción [modern-day Paraguay]); Juan de Ayolas; and Alvar Núñez Cabeza de Vaca (1490–1560), who made the famous overland expedition to Mexico City after the collapse of the Narváez adventure to the southwestern part of the United States in the 1520s.

farther from Spain and have lived longer without order and justice, albeit in all the Indies there never was any order and justice, as one may see from all that has been recounted before.

Among other infinite deeds, those that will be spoken of below have been read in the Council of the Indies:

A tyrannical governor gave orders to certain of his people that they should go to certain Indian villages, and if they were not given food, the Indians should all be slain. And they went under this authority, and since the Indians, as their enemies, would not give them food to eat, more out of fear at seeing them and trying to flee them than from lack of liberality, the Spaniards put above five thousand souls to the sword.

Furthermore, a certain number of peaceable Indians came to them, whom they had happened to send for, and the Indians put themselves in their hands and offered to serve them. And either because these poor wretches did not come soon enough or because it is the Spaniards' vulgar wont and custom, they resolved to plant in them a dreadful fear and horror of them, and the governor ordered that they should all be delivered over to another nation of Indians, who were their sworn enemies. And the peaceable Indians, weeping and pleading, begged that they be put to death by the Spaniards rather than delivered over to their enemies. And refusing to come out of the house in which they were being kept, they were hacked to pieces where they stood, pleading and saying: "We came to serve you in peace, and you kill us; our blood remains upon these walls in witness of our unjust death and your cruelty." A remarkable deed was this, in truth, and worthy of consideration, and much more of lamentation.

On the Great Kingdoms and Great Provinces of Perú

In the year 1531, another great tyrant[118] went with a number of people to the kingdoms of Perú, where, entering with the same title and intention and principles that all others in the past had also had (for he was one of those who had most fiercely laboured and for the longest time in all the cruelties and devastations that had been wrought in Terra Firma, since the year 1510), he did greatly increase the cruelties and slaughters and robberies and thefts, without faith or truth, destroying villages, lay-

---

[118] Francisco Pizarro (1475–1541), who died in the civil wars among the Spanish governors in Peru following the capture and death of the Inca emperor Atahualpa. The New Laws (see p. 98 in this edition) make specific reference to this terrible period and the ravages that were committed.

ing waste, murdering their people, and being the cause of such heinous evils in those lands that we are certain than no one man is sufficient to recount them and weigh them, until we see them and know them clearly on the Day of Judgment. And with respect to some of those I wish to tell, their deformity and the qualities and circumstances that distort them and increase their gravity and make them hideously monstrous, truly I will not be capable of weighing.

In making his accursed *entrada* he committed and caused many murders and destroyed divers villages and stole a large quantity of gold. On one island that is near those same provinces, named Pugna,[119] most populous and gracious, he and his men were received by the lord and people of it like angels from heaven, yet after six months, the Spaniards having eaten all their provisions and the Indians once again uncovering[120] the stores of wheat[121] that they had for themselves and their women and children in times of drought and sterility, and offering this to them with many tears, that they should consume it and eat it at their will, the coin with which the Spaniards paid them in the end was that they put them to the sword and ran great numbers of the people of that island through with their spears and lances, and those whom they could take alive, they made them slaves with other great and singular cruelties that they committed upon them, leaving almost the entire island without people.

From there, they went to the province of Tumbala,[122] which is on Terra Firma, and they slew and destroyed all there that they could. And because all the people fled from their heinous and dreadful deeds, they said that they had risen in revolt and were rebels against the king. This tyrant had a certain ruse: Those to whom he made petition and those who came to give him presents of gold and silver and all that they had, he would tell them to bring more, until he saw that either they had no more or brought no more, and then he would say that he would receive them as vassals of the king and queen of Spain, and he would embrace them and order his men to blow two trumpets that he had, giving them to understand that from that time onward, they would take no more from them nor do them any harm, albeit holding as their legal chattel all that they had stolen from them and all that the Indians had given

---

[119] Today "Puna," in the Gulf of Guayaquil, southern Ecuador.

[120] Opening, unsealing.

[121] Corn; although the native-American word *maíz* had begun to enter the Spanish language when this account was written, and has been used by Las Casas several times before this in these pages, here he uses the European word *trigo*, wheat.

[122] Túmbez.

them out of fear, for they had heard terrible tidings of the Spaniards before they were taken under the aid and protection of the king. As
though after thus being received under the royal protection they were
not oppressed, robbed, devastated, and destroyed, and as though it were
not he who at last destroyed them in this wise.

A few days afterward, the universal king and emperor of those kingdoms, who was called Atabálipa,[123] came to where he was, and he came
with many naked people and their laughable weapons, not knowing
how swords cut and lances wounded, and how swiftly horses ran, and
who the Spaniards were (who if the devils themselves had gold, the
Spaniards would rush at them like wolves to steal it from them), and he
came to the place where the Spaniards were, saying "Where are those
Spaniards? Come out here. I shall not move from this place until I obtain satisfaction for the vassals of mine that have been slain, and the villages that have been razed to the ground and rendered unhabited, and
the riches that have been stolen from me." And the Spaniards came out
to him and slew infinite numbers of his people, taking as their prisoner
this king who had come on a litter; and when he was their prisoner, they
treated for his ransom. He promised to give four million *castellanos,* and
he gave fifteen, and they promised to release him. But in the end, keeping neither faith nor their word (as never in the Indies have the
Spaniards kept their word with the Indians), they asked him if by his
order many people would come together, and he answered that in all
that land not a leaf of a tree moved save by his word, and that if people
came together, they might believe that it was by his order, and that he
was a prisoner, and they should slay him. Despite all this, they sentenced him to be burned alive, although later some people entreated
the captain that he should be drowned, and once drowned be burned.
And when the king learned this, he said: "Why are you burning me?
What have I done to you? Did you not promise to release me if I gave
you gold? And did I not give you more than I had pledged to give? Thus
you wanted it, and so now send me to your king in Spain," and many
other things that he said in his great confusion and his detestation of the
Spaniards' terrible injustice. And in the end they did burn him. Consider here the justice and title of this war, the imprisonment of this lord,
and the sentence and execution of his death, and the full knowledge
with which those tyrants stole such great treasures in those kingdoms,
from that grand king and from infinite other lords and subjects.

---

[123] This is Atahualpa, the great king captured and murdered, as Las Casas notes, in
Cajamarca.

Of an infinite number of deeds remarkable in malice and cruelty directed at extirpating those peoples from the earth and committed by those who call themselves Christians, I will recount here only a few which a friar of the order of Saint Francis saw at the beginning, and signed them with his name, sending communications from those parts and others to these kingdoms of Castile, and I have in my power a communication with his own signature, which reads in part as follows:

I, Fray Marcos de Niza, of the order of Saint Francis, commissary over the friars of that same order in the provinces of Perú, being one of the first men of the cloth who with the first Christians entered into those provinces, do hereby declare, giving true witness of some things which I with my own eyes saw in that land, in greatest part concerning the treatment and conquests made of the native inhabitants thereof:

Firstly, that I am an eye-witness, and by true experience did learn and comprehend that those Indians of Perú are the most benevolent people that have been seen of all the Indians, and are a friend and companion to the Christians. And I saw that they would give gold and silver and gems to the Spaniards in abundance, and whatever they might be asked that they possessed, and all good service; and never did the Indians come out to make war, but rather peace, so long as they were not given occasion by ill treatment and cruelties; rather, they would receive the Spaniards with all benevolence and honour into their villages, and give them food and as many male and female slaves as they asked, to serve them.

Furthermore, that I am witness and do hereby testify that without those Indians giving cause or occasion to the Spaniards, when the Spaniards entered into their lands and after their great cacique, Atabaliba, had given above two million in gold to them and had given all the land in his power without resistance, they did burn said Atabaliba, who was the lord of all the land, and after him burned alive his captain-general Cochilimaca, who had come in peace to the governor with other high persons. And in the same manner, within a few days after these they burned Chamba, another very high lord of the province of Quito, without reason or cause whatever.

In likewise they burned Chapera, a lord of the Canaries,[124] unjustly. And likewise Alvis, one of the greatest lords there was in Quito, they burned his feet and gave him many other torments so that he would tell where the gold of Atabaliba was, about which treasure (it seemed) he knew naught. Likewise in Quito they burned Cozopanga, who was governor of all the provinces of Quito. And Cozopanga, owing to certain petitions, or demands, made on him by Sebastián de Benalcázar, the

---

[124] De Niza seems to have confused the islands off Spain with the Cañari people of south-central Ecuador, where today there is the town of Cañar.

governor's captain, came in peace, and because he did not give as much gold as they asked, they burned him and many other caciques and high persons. And so far as I can understand, the Spaniards purposed that no lord be left alive in all that realm.

Furthermore, the Spaniards gathered up a great number of Indians and closed them up in three large houses, as many as would fit inside, and they set fire to them and burned them all, without the Indians having done the least thing to any Spaniard or giving the slightest cause. And it fell out there that a cleric named Ocaña pulled a boy out of the fire as he was burning, and another Spaniard came along and took him by the hands and threw him into the midst of the flames, where he was burned to ashes like the rest. And this Spaniard who had thrown the Indian into the fire in that wise, that same day, returning to the camp, fell dead on the road, and it seems to me that he was not buried.

Furthermore, I do declare that I myself saw with my own eyes the Spaniards cut off the hands, noses, and ears of male and female Indians, with no reason save that they desired to do so, and in so many places and parts that it would be too long to tell. And I saw that the Spaniards would turn dogs on the Indians, to tear them to pieces, and I saw many attacked by dogs in this wise. Likewise, I saw so many houses and villages burned that I would not be able to tell the number, so many were there. Likewise it is true that they seized suckling babies by their arms and threw them as far as they were able, and committed other outrages and cruelties for no reason, which filled me with horror, and countless other deeds that I saw, which would be too long to tell.

Furthermore, I saw them call the caciques and Indians of great estate[125] who came no doubt in peace and, promising them safety, no sooner would they come than the Spaniards burn them. And in my presence, they burned two: one in Andón[126] and the other in Tumbala, and I was unable to prevent it, no matter how much I preached. And by God and my conscience, so far as I can know, for no other reason than these cruel deeds and treatments, and for the good cause they have been given, as may be clear to any man, the Indians of Perú are risen in revolt and rebellion.[127] For they have been told no truth, no word to them has been kept, but rather, against all reason and justice, they and all their land have been destroyed, and such deeds done unto them that they have resolved that they would prefer to die than suffer such outrages.

Furthermore, I declare that by the accounting of the Indians, there is much more gold hidden than revealed, and this gold, because of the in-

---

[125] Of high rank, position, or title.

[126] *Sic*, for Ancón.

[127] The revolt of 1537–1538 led by the great Inka leader Tupac Amaru.

justices and cruelties that the Spaniards have wrought, they have refused to reveal, nor will they, so long as they are met with such treatment, and they will prefer to die like those who have gone before. In which actions God Our Lord has been greatly offended, and His Majesty done great disservice and disappointed in the loss of this land, which might well have yielded food for all Castile yet will, in my opinion, be extremely difficult, labourious, and costly to recover.

All of these are the words of that friar, most formal, and are signed also by the bishop of México,[128] giving witness that all this was declared by said father, Fray Marcos.

Here it must be considered what this priest says he saw, because it was all within fifty or an hundred leagues of land, and nine or ten years ago, for it was at the beginning and there were very few Spaniards at that time, though at the sound of gold four or five thousand Spaniards later went and spread through many great kingdoms and provinces for above five hundred and seven hundred leagues, and they have left them now full devastated, perpetrating these deeds and others more savage yet, and cruel. Truly, from that day to this, above a thousand times more souls have been destroyed and devastated than have been counted, and with less fear of God and the king, nor any pity, they have destroyed a great part of the lineage of humankind. More are now gone and have been slain in those kingdoms to this day (and today are still being slain) in a space of ten years, than four million souls.

A few days ago, they killed a great queen by running her through with a lance. This was the wife of the Inga,[129] he who was left as king in those kingdoms, and who the Christians, through their tyrannies, laying hands on him, made him rise in revolt, and so he is now against them. And they took the queen, his wife, and against all justice and reason, slew her (and it is even said that she was with child), for no cause but to give pain to her husband.

If one were to tell all the particular cruelties and slaughters that the Christians in those kingdoms of Perú have committed and every day go on committing, without any doubt they would inspire horror and reprehension, and so many would there be, that all we have said in other places would be overpassed and seem small, so many and so grave are they.

---

[128] Fray Juan de Zumárraga.
[129] *Sic*, for Inka/Inca; the king was Mango Inka.

On the New Kingdom of Granada[130]

In the year 1539, there was a confluence of many tyrants at once, going out from Venezuela and from Santa Marta and from Cartagena to seek Perú; and others who from Perú itself moved downward, to penetrate and pass into those lands, and they found, beyond Santa Marta and Cartagena, three hundred leagues inland, a number of exceedingly fertile and admirable provinces, filled with infinite numbers of people as docile and tractable and good as all the others, and wealthy, too, in gold and those gems they call emeralds.[131] And they gave those lands the name the New Kingdom of Granada, because the tyrant[132] who first came to those lands was born in this kingdom here of Granada.[133] And because many iniquitous and cruel men such as those who in the Indies gather from all parts were most particularly accomplished butchers and spillers of human blood, most used and experienced in the great sins, spoken of above, that abound in many parts of the Indies, for that reason their hellish and demonic deeds have been so many and so abominable, and so dreadful the circumstances and qualities that uglify them and increase their gravity, that they have far exceeded others of the kind, and even those that others and they themselves in those same provinces have done and committed.

Of the infinite number that they have perpetrated in these three years, and which even to this day they have not ceased doing, I will tell very briefly only some: That against a Spanish governor of their own (because he refused to allow anyone in that New Kingdom of Granada to rob and kill, so that he himself might rob and kill) a trial was held, with many witnesses, regarding the devastations and outrages and slaughters that he had done and was still doing, and this was read and is now today in the Council of the Indies.

The witnesses in that trial do attest that all that kingdom was at peace and serving the Spaniards, with the Indians giving the Spaniards food from their labours constantly, and tilling their fields and doing other things, and bringing them much gold and gems, emeralds, and all that they had and could, and with the villages and lords and people of those

---

[130] New Granada was modern-day Colombia, especially around Bogotá.

[131] In using the phrase "which they *call* emerald," Las Casas would seem either to be unfamiliar with the name of this gemstone or to have seen it applied to another sort of stone than the one found abundantly in Peru and other places in Central and South America.

[132] Jiménez de Quesada.

[133] The reader is reminded that Las Casas is writing this treatise in Spain.

lands having been divided among themselves by the Spaniards[134] (which is the means they employ toward their ultimate end, which is gold), and all of them having been brought under the wonted hand of tyranny and bondage, the tyrannical captain-major who ruled that land ordered that the king and lord of all that kingdom be taken, and he held him prisoner full six or seven months, demanding gold and emeralds without any reason or cause whatsoever. And this king, who was called Bogotá,[135] owing to the fear that they instilled in him, said that he would give a house of the gold that they asked of him, expecting to be released from the hand of the one who so afflicted and tormented him, and he sent Indians to bring gold; and several times they brought a great quantity of gold and gems, but since he did not give them a house of gold, the Spaniards ordered that he be killed, because he had not kept his word. The tyrant instructed the others to ask for that judgment before him. And they did ask it in a trial, accusing that king of all that land; and the captain-major sat in judgement, sentencing him to torture if he did not give that house of gold. And they tortured him with the *strappado*[136] and then they poured boiling fat upon his belly, shackled him by his feet to irons atop one stake, with his neck bound to another, and two men tugging at his hands, and while he was in this position they held fire to his feet; and the tyrant would enter from time to time and tell him that he would die in that wise, little by little, by torture, if he did not give up the gold. And the captain kept his word and killed this lord with tortures. And while he was torturing him, God gave a sign of His detestation of those cruelties by burning all the village in which the torments were perpetrated.

All the other Spaniards, both to imitate their good captain and because they know no other thing than to hack those poor souls to pieces, did the same, torturing them with divers savage torments each one, the cacique and lord of the village or villages that were within their *encomendado*, even while those lords and all their peoples were serving them and giving them as much gold and emeralds as they could and as they had. And they tortured them only that they might give more gold and gems than they already gave them. And so they burned and dismembered all the lords of that land.

[134] By *encomienda* (see Glossary).

[135] *Sic*, for Bacatá.

[136] As the name might lead one to surmise, this is an Italian torture, which consists of hoisting the victim by a rope, generally by his arms tied behind his back, and dropping him from a height without allowing him to strike the ground.

Out of fear of the consummate cruelties that one of the particular tyrants committed upon the Indians, a great lord called Daitama ran away into the wilderness with many of his people, fleeing so much inhumanity. Because they have at least this means of refuge and aid (if they are able to do it), although the Spaniards call this act rebellion and revolt and uprising. When the tyrannical captain-major learned of this escape, he sent people to that cruel man whose ferocity had driven the Indians (peaceable folk but subjected to such terrible tyranny and evildoing) into the wilderness, and this man went off to search for them, and it availed the Indians naught that they had hid themselves in the bowels of the earth, for the Spaniards found a great number of people, and they killed and dismembered above five hundred souls, men and women and children, for they pardoned none. And the witnesses attest that that same lord Daitama, before those people killed him, came to that cruel man and brought him four or five thousand *castellanos*, and still the cruel captain carried out this devastation I have painted above.

Another time, a great number of people came to serve the Spaniards, and did serve them with the humility and simplicity that is their wont; and though feeling themselves secure, the captain came one night to the city where the Indians were serving, and he ordered that all those kingdoms be put to the sword, while they were sleeping and some of them eating supper and resting from their day's labours. And he did this because it seemed to him meet to commit that outrage, to sow fear in all the people of that land.

Another time the captain ordered that all the Spaniards swear to the number of caciques and high persons and common folk that each one had in service in his house, and that they then be brought to the plaza, and there he ordered that all their heads be cut off, and there they killed four hundred or five hundred souls. And the witnesses say that he thought in this wise to pacify the land.

Of a certain tyrannical person, albeit not in the service of the king, it is said by witnesses that he wrought great acts of cruelty, killing and cutting off many hands and noses of men and women both, and destroying many people.

Another time the captain sent that same cruel man with certain Spaniards to the province of Bogotá to discover who was the lord who had succeeded in that realm, after he had tortured to death the universal lord, and he made his way through many leagues of land, taking all the Indians that he found; and because they would not tell him who the lord was that had succeeded, some he had the hands cut off and others he ordered thrown to savage dogs that tore them to pieces, both women and men, and in this wise he killed and destroyed many Indians, both male and female. And one day, at about the fourth watch of the day,[137] he came upon some Indian caciques or captains and many common folk who were at peace and unwitting of any evil, for he had assured them and given his word that they would receive from him no harm or evil, and in that security they came down out of the thorny wilderness where they had been hiding, to the cleared ground where they had their village. And in that wise, fearing not for their safety, but rather secure in their trust of the word they had been given, he took a great number of those people, women and men alike, and ordered them to lay their hand outstretched upon the ground, and he himself, with his short saber he cut off their hands, and told them that he punished them in that manner because they would not tell him where the new lord was who had succeeded in that kingdom.

Another time, because the Indians did not give him a coffer filled with gold, . . . they killed an infinite number of souls, and cut off the hands and noses of count- less women and men, and others they threw to the savage dogs, who ate them and tore them to pieces.

[137] Just at dusk, or sunset.

Another time, because the Indians did not give him a coffer filled
with gold, which this cruel captain had asked them for, he sent people
to wage war against them, and they killed an infinite number of souls,
and cut off the hands and noses of countless women and men, and others they threw to the savage dogs, who ate them and tore them to pieces.

Another time, the Indians in a certain province in that kingdom seeing that the Spaniards had burned three or four high lords, they went for
fear up onto a strong cliff, or precipice, where they might defend themselves from enemies so wanting in all the affections of humankind, and
they were upon the cliff and they were (so the witnesses say) four or five
thousand Indians. And this same captain sent a great and remarkable
tyrant (one who overpasses all the many tyrants that in those parts have
wrought destruction), accompanied with certain other Spaniards, so
that he might punish the *rebellious* Indians, as they called them, who
were fleeing from such terrible pestilence and butchery, as though they
had done some unjust thing and it belonged to those Spaniards to mete
out punishment and take vengeance, as though the Indians were deserving of any torture, however bloody and pitiless, for so lacking are
they in pity for those innocents. And when the Spaniards came to this
precipice, they ascended it by force, for the Indians were naked and unarmed; and they called out to the Indians at peace, and they assured
them that they would do them no harm, beseeching them not to fight,
and so the Indians held off. And this bloodthirsty captain ordered the
Spaniards in full force to take the cliff, and when they had taken it, to attack the Indians. And the tigers and lions set upon the gentle sheep and
ripped their bellies open and put them to the sword, so many that they
had to stop to rest, for they had hacked so many Indians to pieces. After
having rested a while, the captain ordered them to slay and cast over
that precipice, which was very high, all those who were still alive. And
so they cast them all onto the rocks below, and the witnesses say that
they beheld a rain of Indians thrown from the cliff down to the ground,
some seven hundred men who fell, and were broken into pieces.

And to consummate all their great cruelty, they sought out all the Indians who had hidden in the plants and underbrush, and he ordered
that they all be run through with lances and knives, and so they were
slain and cast over the cliff. And still he would not be content with such
cruel acts, for he was of a mind to impress fear even more strongly in the
Indians' hearts, and eke to increase the iniquitousness of his sins, and so
he ordered that all the Indians, both women and men, that his soldiers
had taken alive (for each one in those attacks is wont to choose some
male and female Indians and young boys to serve him) be closed into a
house of straw (with those that were best to serve chosen and left be-

hind) and fire set to it, and so they burned them alive, some forty or fifty. Others he ordered thrown to the savage dogs, which tore them to pieces and ate them.

Another time, this same tyrant went to a certain village called Cota, and he laid hands on many Indians and suffered the dogs to tear fifteen or twenty lords and high-ranking men to pieces, and cut off many women's and men's hands, and tied them to ropes and tethered the ropes between two poles, so that the other Indians might see what he had done to them. In that there were some seventy pairs of hands, and he cut off many women's and children's noses.

The deeds and cruelties done by this man, this enemy of God, in that land and all the province of Guatimala, and indeed wheresoe'er he went—these acts, I say, no man might understand or explain, because first, they are innumerable, and second, never before heard of or seen done. And it is many years now that he has been in those lands, committing those deeds and burning and laying waste and destroying those nations and lands.

Further witnesses in this trial do attest that so many and so great have been the cruelties and murders that have been done and still today are being done in that New Kingdom of Granada by those captains in their very persons and also, consented to by all those tyrants and destroyers of the human race and done by those who are with them, that they have the entire land laid waste and lost, and if Your Majesty does not soon order that this be remedied (for the slaughter of the Indians is carried out for no reason but to get gold from them, which they do not have, for all they once had they have given up), order that this slaughter be ended in a short time, I say, then there shall be no Indians to sustain the land, and all will be waste and desert and without inhabitants.

Here should be noted the cruel and pestilential tyranny of those wretched tyrants, how harsh and vehement and diabolic it has been, to such degree that in a space of two years or three since that kingdom was discovered (which, so say all those who have been there and the witnesses of that trial did also attest, was the most populous land that might exist on earth), they have slain and depopulated it all, without pity or fear of God and the king, and if in a short time Your Majesty does not put an end to those hellish deeds, there will not remain a man or woman alive. And this I myself do believe, because I have seen with my own eyes many great lands in those parts, and in very few days they have been destroyed and left without a soul to live upon them.

There are other great provinces that border parts of that New Kingdom of Granada, which are called Popayán and Cali, and another three or four that possess above five hundred leagues. They have been devastated and destroyed in the same wise and manners as those others, the Spaniards robbing and torturing to death and committing all the infinite aforesaid outrages upon the people there. Because the land once was exceedingly fertile, and those who now return from there say that it is a great pity and most grievous to see so many and such great villages burned and devastated, for where there was a village of one thousand and two thousand villagers, they did not find fifty, and others were burned utterly to the ground and without a soul. And in many places they would find one and two hundred leagues and three hundred, all without a soul, with great villages burned to the ground and destroyed. And finally, from the kingdoms of Perú through the province of Quito there went great and cruel tyrants, penetrating the land to that very New Kingdom of Granada and Popayán and Cali, through Cartagena and Urabá,[138] and from Cartagena other accursed tyrants went out toward Quito, and then afterward others through the lands of the Río de San Juan, which is on the coast of the Southern Ocean[139] (and all of these met and came together), and they have laid waste and extirpated every soul for above six hundred leagues of land, casting those immense numbers of souls into hell, and acting in the same wise today to the miserable, though innocent, people who remain.

And to prove that the rule I set forth at the beginning might be seen to be true, that the tyranny and violence and injustices wrought by the Spaniards against those gentle lambs and sheep grew greater in harshness and inhumanity and evil-doing day by day, what now is done in those provinces (among other things more than meriting all the fires and torments) is the following: After the deaths and devastations of the wars, they bound the people, as we have said, into most grievous servitude, and one cast two hundred Indians to the demons, another cast three hundred. The diabolical *comendero*, they say, sent for an hundred Indians to come before him; and they came like lambs; and when they had come, he ordered that thirty or forty of them have their heads cut off, and says to the others: "I shall do the same to you all, if you do not serve me well or if you leave without my licence."

And consider here for love of God, all those who may read this, what manner of deed this is, and whether it does not exceed all the cruelty

[138] That is, along the Gulf of Darien.

[139] Here, and generally in Spanish, the Pacific. When Las Casas is speaking specifically about the Caribbean islands, however, "Southern Ocean" refers to the Caribbean, which lies south of the Antilles archipelago.

and injustice that may be thought or conceived, and whether it does not befit those Christians to be called devils, and whether it would not be better to commend the Indians to the devils and the fires of Hell at once than to these Christians of the Indies.

And another thing I would say, and that is that I do not know which is more cruel and more hellish, and more filled with the ferocity and savagery of wild beasts—that which I have told above or that which I am about to tell. It has been often said above that the Spaniards of the Indies have fierce, angry dogs trained to kill the Indians and tear them to pieces. And I would say to all persons who are true Christians, and even those who are not, to think whether such a thing has been heard of in all the world, that to maintain those dogs, they bring many Indians in chains with them on the journeys they take, as though they were herds of pigs, and they kill them and have a public butchery of human flesh, and some say to the others: "Lend me a haunch of that rogue there to give my dogs until I kill another one," as though they were lending haunches of pork or legs of lamb. There are others who go out a-hunting of a morning with their dogs, and when they return for dinner and are asked how the hunting went, they reply: "Good, good, because I have left fifteen or twenty of those rogues dead with my dogs."[140] All these things and other diabolical deeds are now proved in trials that some of the tyrants have brought against others. What can be more hideous and savage and inhumane than this?

And with this, I will close, until news of more egregious evil-doing comes (if worse there can be than this), or until we return there ourselves to see them again, as we have incessantly been seeing now for forty-two years with our own eyes, protesting upon God and my conscience that, as I believe and hold as a surety, so many and so great are the perditions, harms, destructions, devastations, deaths and most terrible cruelties, and so vast the depopulation, and so heinous the violent, unjust deeds, the robberies and slaughters that have been done upon those nations and those lands (and are still being done this day in all those parts of the Indies), that in all the things that I have said and all the things that I have weighed and measured, I have not said or weighed, in quantity or quality, the ten-thousandth part of what has been done and is still being done this day.

And so that any Christian may have more compassion yet for those innocent nations and their perdition and so that their condemnation may be more grievous to us, and more blame and abomination and

---

[140] That is, they hunted Indians with dogs, for sport.

detestation for their greed and ambition and cruelty fall upon the Spaniards, I would have every person know this undeniable truth, along with those others which I have set forth above: That from the time the Indies were discovered until this day, never, in any part of them, have the Indians done any wrong or evil to any Christian without first having received wrongs and thefts and acts of treachery from them. At first, they always esteemed them as immortal, come from the sky, or heaven, and as such they received them and took them in, until the Spaniards' works and deeds testified to who they were and what they were about, and what their purpose was.

And it would be well to add one further thing: That since the beginning until this day, the Spaniards have had no more care that faith in Jesus Christ be preached to those people and those nations, than if they were dogs or other beasts. Indeed, they have forbidden men of the cloth to carry out that attempt, with many afflictions and persecutions laid upon them for it, so that they would not preach, for it seemed to the Spaniards that it would be an impediment to the taking of the gold and riches that their greed had promised them. And today in all the Indies, there is no more knowledge of God, whether He is made of wood, or sky, or earth, than there was an hundred years ago among those people, unless it be in New Spain, where men of the cloth have journeyed about, and that is but a small corner of the Indies; and so they all have perished and still today perish without faith and without sacraments.

Testament

I, Fray Bartolomé de las Casas, or Casaus, friar of the order of Saint Dominic, who by the mercy of God am here today in this court of Spain, was persuaded by some notable persons resident in this Court, jealous[141] of God's honour, and compassionate toward the afflictions and calamities of their fellow beings (although I myself had conceived the same purpose but had not put it to work on account of my constant occupations), was persuaded by them I say to set down an accounting of the hell that is the Indies, so that those infinite masses of souls redeemed by the blood of Jesus Christ may not die for all eternity without any help for it, but rather know their Creator and be saved. And by the compassion that I have for my native land, which is Castile, I pray that God not destroy it for the great sins committed against its faith and hon-

[141] Zealous, loving, having care for.

our. I completed this account in Valencia, on the eighth day of December in the year 1542, at a time when all the violence, oppression, tyranny, slaughter, robbery and destruction, outrage, depopulation, anguish, and calamities spoken of above are of terrible force and indeed at their uttermost, wheresoe'er there are Christians in those Indies. Given that in some parts they are more savage and abominable than in others: México and its territory is a little less bad, or at least one dares not do these deeds so publicly in that realm, because there and not in any other place is there some justice (however little it may be). For there, too, they slay the Indians with their infernal tributes.

I have great hope that the emperor and king of Spain, our lord Don Carlos, the fifth of that name, may come to understand (for until now the truth has always been most industriously covered over) the acts of malice and treachery which have been and still are being done upon those nations and lands, against the will of God and his own, and that he may bring an end to so many evils and bring relief to that New World which God has given him, as the lover and cultivator, as he is, of justice. And I pray that his glorious and fertile life and our imperial state, to the aid and benefit of all His universal Church and the final salvation of the king's own soul, be made by God to prosper and increase for many years to come, Amen.

After the account above was written, certain laws and ordinances were published which Your Majesty ordered to be pronounced at that time in the city of Barcelona in the year 1542, in the month of November; and in the city of Madrid, the year after.[142] By which laws and ordinances the order was given, which at that time seemed most right and fitting, that so much evil-doing and sinning against God and our fellow beings and the utter destruction and perdition of that realm be ended. Your Majesty made those laws after many gatherings of persons of great authority, letters,[143] and conscience, and also debates and conferences in the city of Valladolid, and finally with the agreement and consent of all others, who gave their vows in writing, and appealed to the law of Jesus Christ as true Christians and also as men free of corruption and besmirchment by the treasures stolen from the Indies. For those treasures did soil the hands and even more the souls of many who at that time were in authority, which reason explains their blindness in destroying those lands, with no scruples whatsoever of it. And when these

---

[142] These are the famous "New Laws," an excerpt from which is included in this edition, pp. 93–102.

[143] Learning, education.

laws were published, those who did the work of the tyrants (and many of them were at that time within the Court) made and submitted many documents in support of those tyrants their masters (for all these ministers were much aggrieved by those laws, believing that said laws closed the doors to their own participation[144] in the spoils of the Indies), and they sent them out to many parts of the Indies. When they saw those informations, and before the new judges came who were to carry them out, those there who had been given charge of stealing, destroying, and laying waste with their tyrannies, knowing (as is well known and often said) about the sins and violence that those here had supported and maintained, and since they never had law or order of any kind before, but rather all the disorder that Lucifer could sow, those tyrants, I say, made such a noise and clamour that when the good judges went to carry out the laws, these men resolved (since they had lost both fear and love of God) to put aside their shame and obedience to their king. And so they resolved to be known as traitors, being the harsh and savage and unbridled tyrants that they were; and this was especially so in the kingdoms of Perú, where today, in the year 1547, such terrible and appalling and nefarious deeds are done as never were done before in the Indies or in the world, not just upon the Indians, all or almost all of whom are already dead, and upon those lands of theirs which are now unhabited, but even upon one another. And this, I say, is the just judgement of God, for since there has been no justice of the king to punish them, it comes from heaven, allowing some to be the hangmen and executioners of others. And seeing this uprising by those men, in all the other parts of the world, too, other men have refused to obey the laws, and under the colour of appealing them, they are as rebellious as the others, for it galls them to leave the usurped estates and the great haciendas that they own, and open their hands to the Indians, whom they hold in perpetual bondage. For be it known that where they have ceased slaying the Indians with the sword at once, they slay them little by little with services to their persons and other unjust and intolerable vexations. And to this day the king is not powerful enough to put an end to this, because all, large and small, live to steal, some more, some less, some publicly and openly, others secretly and stealthily. And under the guise of serving the king, they dishonour God and rob and destroy the king.

This work was printed in the most noble and most loyal city of Sevilla, in the house of Sebastián Trujillo, bookseller. In the year of Our Lady of Grace MDLII.

---

[144] That is, they would lose their portions of the booty.

From The Laws of Burgos (1512–1513) Royal Ordinances for the Good Government and Treatment of the Indians*

$\mathcal{Q}_{\downarrow\mathcal{O}}$

The Laws of Burgos represented the first attempt at comprehensive colonial legislation by the Spanish for their colony established in Hispaniola in 1502 and beginning to expand to the neighboring Caribbean islands by 1512. They clearly indicated that Spain was serious about establishing an overseas colonial empire of Spanish and non-Spanish peoples, thereby accepting a certain amount of plurality. Apart from regulating the conduct of the Spanish toward the indigenous population, the Laws demonstrated considerable sensitivity to the native populations. The Laws clarified the American usage of encomienda, the allocation of Indians in service to the Spaniards, suggesting that, unlike a mere repartimiento, or arbitrary distribution, the encomienda carried both privileges and responsibilities. Although the Laws attempted to protect the Indians, the Dominican orders considered them inadequate and unenforceable. Las Casas felt that they gave the Spanish settlers too much power over the local inhabitants.

XXIV

Furthermore, we order that no person or persons shall dare to whip or abuse any Indian, or call him dog or any other form of address except his proper name. Likewise, no Indian shall be punished without the

---

*Translated by Franklin W. Knight from Roland D. Hussey, "Text of the Laws of Burgos (1512–1513) concerning the Treatment of the Indians, with an Introduction by Roland D. Hussey," *Hispanic American Historical Review* 12:2 (May 1932): 301–326.

owner of said Indian first bringing him to the *Visitadores* for punishment. The penalty for those who violate this order shall be five gold
pesos for each infraction.

XXV

Furthermore, it has come to our knowledge that many persons who
have Indians in *encomienda* serve us poorly by using them to sow and
cultivate [instead of sending them to the gold mines]. We order and
command that every person having Indians in *encomienda* must provide
one-third (and more than one-third if he so desires) of his allocation [of
Indians] to work in the gold mines under penalty for non-compliance of
three gold pesos for each Indian short of the one-third. We exempt residents of La Sabana and Villanueva de Yaquimo because they live so far
from the mines and order that such exempted Indians be employed in
the manufacture of hammocks and cotton shirts, and the raising of pigs,
or in any other farming activity that benefits the community. Because I
have been informed that some Indians, on moving to the estates of the
settlers, are required to build houses and engage in other necessary activities that prevent the settlers from immediately supplying one-third of
them to the mines, I order you—the said Admiral, judges, and officials—to permit such use as you deem fit provided the exempted time
be as brief as possible.

XXVI

Furthermore, we order and command that those whose estates are so far
from the mines as to make the supplying of provisions to their own Indians [working in the mines] difficult shall place their Indians with those of
nearby estates in order that their Indians may receive provisions. And we
stipulate that the supplier of the distant Indians engage a miner to ensure
their proper maintenance, and that under no circumstances should the
Indians' care be contracted out under the penalty already stipulated.

XXVII

Furthermore, because so many Indians have been brought from the
neighboring islands, with more being brought each day, we order and

command that the Indians shall be properly instructed in the Faith according to the practices on the other islands, that they each be supplied with hammocks and food, and that—except for slaves whose individual treatment remains the responsibility of their masters—they be visited by the *Visitadores*. We order that these Indians be treated without the rigor and harshness of slaves elsewhere, but rather with love and gentleness to incline them more effectively to the practices of our Faith.

XXVIII

Furthermore, we order and command that the estate of any person who abandons his *encomienda* by death (or for any other deserving reason) shall be purchased from his heirs at a fair price established by two persons, under oath, familiar with the estate. These persons should be named by you, the aforesaid Admiral, judges, and officials, to ensure that the Indians are not relocated: those to whom the Indians are given in *encomienda* should be residents of the towns from which the Indians were distributed.

XXIX

Furthermore, we order and command that in each town of said island there shall be two *Visitadores* responsible for overseeing the entire town, including its miners, farms and shepherds. These *Visitadores* shall evaluate how the Indians are being taught in the measures of our Faith, how they are personally treated and kept, and how well their caretakers observe our regulations. We order that they take great care in this matter, and we charge their consciences with it.

XXX

Furthermore, we order and command that *Visitadores* shall be selected and named by you, our aforementioned Admiral, and judges and officials, in the form and manner that seem most appropriate to you, as long as the *Visitadores* are selected from the oldest residents of the towns in which they will function as *Visitadores*. We command that they be given some Indians in *encomienda* over and above their allocation for the office and work that accompanies their responsibility, and

that you—the said Admiral, said judges and said officials—select those
Indians. But it is our will that if these *Visitadores* become derelict in
their duties, or fail to comply with our orders especially as pertaining to
subsistence and hammocks, then such Indians as they hold in *encomienda* should be taken from them.

XXXI

Furthermore, we order and command that said *Visitadores* shall be
obliged to visit the residences of the Indians under their charge twice
per year: once at the beginning of the year and again around midyear.
We also order that one *Visitador* should not visit all the time, but rather
that they should alternate visits so that they both may be familiar with
what the other does in order that everything achieves the requisite diligence.

XXXII

Furthermore, we order and command that said *Visitadores* shall refrain
from taking, or having sent to their houses or estates, any Indians who
have fled from their estates or become lost, or were found elsewhere.
Such Indians should be immediately left in the care of a good individual. But every effort should first be made to seek out the original owner
and return the Indians to him. Failing that, the Indians should be
lodged according to the prevailing regulations until claimed by the
rightful owner. If any such Indians are found in the possession of a *Visitador*, he shall forfeit one of his own Indians to his accuser over and beyond the restoration of the original runaway to the rightful owner.

New Laws of the Indies

The New Laws were promulgated at a time of great crisis, not only in the Americas but also in Spain. In the Americas, intrepid conquistadors had ruthlessly opened up the great mainland empires of Mexico and Peru with their vast reservoirs of precious metals. The Emperor Charles confronted a situation in which his subjects could be richer and more powerful than himself. Hernán Cortés is reported to have shouted once to the monarch that he had given more provinces in the Indies—as the Americas were called—than the emperor had inherited cities in Iberia. Indeed, the emperor's authority was openly challenged in Peru where a civil war between Spaniards began in 1535. Bartolomé de las Casas and the Dominicans were aggressively advocating drastic revisions in the administration of the Indies, even to the point of expelling all nonclerical Spanish. In Europe, Spain had become the champion of the Roman Catholic Church against the Protestants and had begun to wage a continental war against the religious reformers. In addition, doubts about the legitimacy of the Spanish possession of the Americas were growing. The New Laws reflected the moral support of the papal ruling of 1537 that validated Spanish proselytizing in the Americas by declaring that the indigenous inhabitants were indeed rational people and therefore capable of receiving the gospel. It also attempted to meet the Dominican position by outlawing the encomienda—*an instruction that could not be immediately upheld, especially in Mexico. But the New Laws also reflected the deep division between various groups in Spain over the role of church and state in the newly incorporated American lands. The regular clergy, especially the Dominican orders, wanted greater independence and greater control over the Spanish colonists. Some colonists wanted the extension of the Iberian feudal traditions and a greater subordination of the local inhabitants. Advisors to the monarch wanted a strengthening and preservation of royal power without the administrative encumbrances imposed by the Cortes of Castile and Aragon.*

Laws and ordinances newly made by His Majesty for the governments of the Indies and the good treatment and conservation of the Indians: which shall be observed in the council and royal courts in which they

93

do reside: and by all the other governors, judges, and private citizens of
them.

Don Carlos, by divine clemency emperor ever august, king of Germany, *Doña Joanna,* his mother, and that same *Don Carlos,* by the
grace of God, king and queen of Castile, León, Aragon, the two Sicilies,
Jerusalem, Navarre, Granada, Toledo, Valencia, Galicia, Mallorca,
Sevilla, Lerdeña, Córdova, Corsica, Murcia, Jaén, the Algarve, Algeci-
ras, Gibraltar, the Canaries, *the Indies, Islands, and Terra Firma of the
Ocean Sea,* count and countess of Barcelona, lord and lady of Biscayne
and of Molina, duke and duchess of Thens and Neopatria, count and
countess of Rusellón and Lerdeña, duke and duchess of Burgundy and
Brabante, count and countess of Flanders and the Tirol——

To: the most illustrious Prince don Felipe our very dear and beloved
grandson and son, and the Infantes our grandchildren and children,
and to the President, and those of our Council of the Indies and our
viceroys and the presidents and oidores of our *Audiencias* and royal
chanceries of those *above said Indies, islands, and Terra Firma of the
Ocean Sea,* and our governors, high mayors and other justices of them,
and to all the councillors, justices, *regidores,* knights, esquires, officers,
and commoners of all the cities and places of those abovesaid, *our Indies, Islands and Terra Firma of the Ocean Sea,* discovered and to be
discovered; and to any other persons, captains, discoverers, settlers, and
residents dwelling in and being native thereof, in whatsoever state, quality, condition, and preeminence they may be; and those who go or at
some future time may go, and to each and all of you in your places and
jurisdictions to whom this our letter may be shown or its transfer signed
by public scrivener . . . and that which is in it contained or any thing or
part thereof that may touch ye and concern ye, or may concern ye in
any manner,

Greetings and grace to you,

   And know ye: That for many years having had will and intention to
occupy ourselves fully in the things of the Indies, on account of the
great importance of them and also with respect to the service of God our
Lord and the increase of His holy Catholic faith, and in the preservation
of the natives of those parts and the good governance and preservation of
all persons, although we have attempted to rid ourselves of this concern,
it has not been possible, on account of the many constant occupations
that have occurred, from which we have not been able to excuse ourselves, and on account of the absences that from these realms I the King
have made on account of necessary causes known to all, and given that

this frequency of occupations has not ceased in all this present year: *Therefore, We did call* persons of all estates, both prelates and nobles and religious persons and some persons of our Council, to come together and speak to one another, and to treat those things of most importance of which we have had notice and which require our attention, and these things being debated and conferred upon, and in a mature manner, and in the presence of myself the King divers times spoken of and debated, and finally having consulted the opinions of all those so brought together, we have resolved to enact and ordain, and *do hereby ordain* the things hereinafter contained, which in addition to the other ordinances and provisions which at divers times we have commanded to be done, as by them it shall appear, *we do hereby command* that henceforward they be taken for inviolable law.

Whereas one of the most principal things in which the *Audiencias* are to serve us is in taking very special care for the good treatment of the Indians and the preservation of them: *We do command* that they inform themselves always of the excesses and ill-treatments that are or were done to said Indians by governors or particular persons, and in what manner the ordinances and instructions that have been given them, and that for the good treatment of them are hereby given, have been and are observed, and in so far as those instructions may have been exceeded or may in future be exceeded, said *Audiencias* shall take care to remedy those treatments by punishing the guilty with all severity and rigour consonant with justice, and ensure that in the suits at law or other matters between the Indians and themselves they employ not ordinary trials or long trials, as is wont to happen on account of the malice of some lawyers and State's attorneys, but rather that the dispute be summarily decided, observing the ways and customs of said Indians, so long as they be not clearly unjust, and that in said *Audiencias* care be taken that lower judges also be apprised of the above-commanded.

Item:[1] *We do order and command* that from this time forward, no cause of war or other reason, even under title of rebellion or for rescue or in any other manner, shall justify making a slave of any Indian whatsoever, and that it is our will that they be treated as subjects of the Crown of Castile, for so they are.

No person may employ the Indians as personal servants . . . or in any other way against their will.

And as we have commanded that henceforward no Indian may in any way be made a slave, *so too* respecting those who until now have

---

[1] Legal terminology for "furthermore," "in addition."

been made so against all reason and law, and against the provisions and instructions given: **We do order and command** that the *Audiencias*, calling the parties without judicial form, but rather summarily and briefly, in order to find the truth, shall set said Indians at liberty, even if the persons who hold them as slaves show the title by which they lawfully have and possess them; and **So that**, lacking persons who may make request of the aforementioned action, the Indians not unjustly remain slaves: **We do command** that the *Audiencias* shall appoint persons who shall pursue this cause for the Indians, and that they be paid from the moneys of the Exchequer and that they be men of trust and diligence.

Item: **We do command** that respecting the burthening of said Indians, the *Audiencias* shall take special care that they be not burthened, or in case this cannot in some parts be excused, it shall be in such manner that said Indians shall suffer no danger to their lives, health, or preservation from immoderate burthening, and that no case of said burthening be permitted against their will and without wages, and that any person who may act contrary to this command shall be punished most severely, and that in this there shall be no remission with respect to any person whatsoever.

Whereas we have been informed in a certain Account that the fishing for pearls has been done without due and appropriate good order, and that it has led to the deaths of many Indians and Negros: **We do command** that no free Indian shall be taken to said fishery against his will, under pain of death, and that whatever bishop and judge there may be in Venezuela shall order whatsoever they think meet so that the slaves who are now in said fishery, both Indian and Negro, shall be preserved, and their deaths ended. And if it appear that said Indians and Negros cannot be spared the danger of death, the fishing for said pearls shall cease, for we hold in much higher esteem—as is only just and reasonable—the preservation of lives than the interest that may come to us from the pearls.

Whereas the viceroys, governors, and their lieutenants, and our officers and prelates, monasteries, hospitals, and houses, both of religion and of currency and exchange, and the Exchequer of those last named, and the offices of our hacienda and other persons favoured by reason of said offices, having had Indians under their *encomienda*, disorders have occurred respecting the treatment of said Indians: **It is our will, and we do so command,** that under our royal Crown be placed all the Indians that are owned and possessed, under any title and cause whatsoever, by those who were or are viceroys, governors, or their lieutenants, or any officer of ours whatever, both of justice and of our possessions, prelates, houses of religion or of our State, hospitals, brotherhoods and guilds, or other similar bodies, even should the Indians have been given in *encomienda* to them by reason of their offices; and even though said officers or governors declare that they wish to leave those offices or governances and retain the Indians, this shall not avail them, nor shall they decline to obey that which we have commanded.

And moreover: **We do command** that all persons who have Indians without possessing title, but who rather have entered into possession of them by their authority, those persons shall be quit of said Indians and said Indians shall be placed under the protection of our royal Crown.

And whereas we are informed that in the case of other persons, even those with title, the *repartimientos* that have been given them are excessive: **We do command** that the *Audiencias*, each in its jurisdiction, shall inform themselves well of this, and in all brevity, and that they lessen said *repartimientos* to those persons to an honest and moderate quantity, and that the rest be placed under our royal Crown; and should any appeal or supplication be interposed by said persons with respect to the acts of said *Audiencias:* **We command** that we be sent a relation of said appeals and supplications with all brevity, so that we may be apprised of the manner in which our command is obeyed; and that in New Spain especially, a judgement be made upon the Indians possessed by Joan Infante and Diego de Ordas and Maestre Roa and Francisco Vasquez de Coronado and Francisco Maldonado and Bernardino Vázquez de Tapia and Joan Xaramillo and Martín Vázquez and Gil Gonzáles de Venavides and many other persons, who are said to hold a very excessive number of Indians, to judge by the information that we have been given; *And whereas* we are informed that there are some persons in said New Spain who are among the first *conquistadores* and have no *repartimiento* of Indians whatsoever: **We command** that the president and *oidores* of said New Spain inform themselves of the persons of this kind, and that they be paid the tribute which they are thus owed for the Indians taken from them, what the president and *oidores* think reasonable for the moderate sustenance and honest entertainment[2] of said first *conquistadores* who are thus without *repartimientos*.

So also, said *Audiencias* shall inform themselves of the manner in which the Indians have been treated by the persons who have had them in *encomienda*, and if they believe that in fairness those persons ought be deprived of them on account of the excesses and ill-treatments that they have done them: **We do command** that said Indians be taken from

---

[2] Sustenance, maintenance, especially of persons in the state or monarch's service.

them and placed under our royal Crown, and with respect to those in Perú, that the viceroy and *Audiencia* inform themselves of the excesses done and the things that have occurred between governors Pizarro and Almagro, and that we be sent a relation of said events, and that the principal persons who most notably shall be found guilty in those revolutions shall have the Indians they possess taken from them and placed under our royal Crown.

And We do furthermore order and command that no viceroy, governor, *Audiencia*, discoverer, or any other person may henceforth possess Indians in *encomienda* through any new provision or through any renunciation or donation or sale or any other manner whatever, nor through vacancy or inheritance, but rather should the person who owns said Indians die, those Indians shall be placed under our royal Crown, and the *Audiencias* shall be charged with informing themselves of all persons who die, and the rank and quality of those persons, and their merits and services, and the manner in which they treated said Indians whom they possessed, and whether the deceased left a wife and children or other heirs, and that we be sent that relation and the quality of the Indians and the land, so that we may command whatever may be required for our service, and show such favour as we think meet for the wife and children of the deceased; and if meanwhile it may seem to the *Audiencia* meet that said wife and children be provided with some sustenance, that may be done from the tributes paid by said Indians, giving said wife and children some moderate amount, the Indians being under the protection of our crown, as we have commanded.

Item: We do order and command that our abovementioned presidents and *oidores* take great care that the Indians who in any manner above-enumerated be taken away and despoiled be very well treated, and instructed in the things of our holy Catholic faith. And as free subjects of ourselves, this shall be the principal care of those presidents and *oidores*, and that which we shall most take account of and that in which we most require that we be obeyed. And they shall provide that they be governed in justice, in the manner and order that the Indians under our royal Crown are governed today in New Spain.

And whereas it is meet that those who have served in the discoveries of those Indies, and also those who aid the population of the Indies and have their wives there, that they be first in the preferences, we do command that our viceroys, presidents, and *oidores* of our *Audiencias* in those places shall, in the provisions of the corrections and other manifestations of our approval, show due preference to any of the first *conquistadores* and afterward those of the married settlers who are persons fit for that, and until those aforenamed be provided as we have commanded, no other person whatsoever shall be provided.

Whereas there having been great inconveniences in our Spaniards suing Indians: *It is our will, and We do so command,* that from this time forward, no claims of this kind shall be heard, whether in the Indies or in our Council of the Indies, whether respecting Indians who are under our Crown or those possessed by a third party, but rather that any matter which of this kind might be solicited be remitted to ourselves, so that when all due information has been taken we may order judgement in the matter; and any demand or suit concerning this matter there might be at the present time, either in our Council of the Indies or in the Indies proper, or in any other place, **We do command** that it be suspended and that no more of it be heard, but rather that the suit be sent to us.

Whereas one of the things that we have been informed is the cause of great disorder, and which in the future may also be, is the manner of the discoveries: **We do order and command** that in said discoveries the following order shall be observed: That he who would discover something by sea shall request license to do so from the *Audiencia* of that district and jurisdiction, and once having it, he may discover and rescue said land, so long as he not bring from the Indies or that Terra Firma that he hath discovered, any Indian whatever, to be sold for a slave, and so be it also (save three or four persons for tongues[3]) for one who wishes to come of his own will, under pain of death, and no person may be taken, nor may any act be done, against the will of the Indians, save for rescue and in the sight of the person whom the *Audiencia* shall name for that purpose, and the order and instruction that the *Audiencia* gives shall be observed, under pain of loss of all possessions and the person becoming subject to our mercy, and said discoverer shall hereby be instructed that in all parts whereinever he may go, he shall take possession in our name, and act always in the highest fashion.

Item, That said discoverer shall, after his discovery, inform the *Audiencia* of whatever he may have done and discovered, and the full relation which the *Audiencia* has taken, that relation shall be sent to our Council of the Indies so that said Council may order whatever may be required respecting the service of God and of ourselves; and said discoverer shall be charged with the population of that place he hath discovered (if he be a fit person for that) or be paid the thanks for that

---

[3] I.e., translators, interpreters.

which he hath served ourselves in it, according to the manner and degree he hath worked and merited and spent, and the *Audiencia* shall send
with each discoverer one or two approved religious persons, and if said
religious persons wish to remain in the discovered land, they may do so.

Item, That no viceroy or governor may sit in any judgement whatsoever regarding new discoveries, whether by sea or land, owing to the inconveniences that follow upon one single person being both governor
and discoverer.

Item, *Whereas* inhabitations and letters-patent have been taken and
done by some persons who intend at the present time to go a-discovering:
It is our will, and we do so command, that in all such discoveries the
provisions contained in these ordinances shall be observed, and even
more so the instructions that the *Audiencias* may give, so long as they be
not contrary to that which we ourselves have ordered and commanded,
and this, regardless of any letters-patent that may have been given; ad-
vising them, that if they do not so observe the provisions aforesaid, or if
they commit excesses, they shall, ipso facto, be suspended from their
posts and be subject to loss of all the mercies that they have enjoyed
from us and all other persons under our mercy, and we command the
Audiencias and each one of them in their district and jurisdiction, that
said discoverers be given the instructions that the *Audiencia* deems
meet, in accordance with that which they may infer from our intention,
as we have ordered, so that said discoveries may with more justice be
carried out and so that the Indians may be well treated and preserved
and instructed in the things of our holy faith and that said discoverers
shall always take special care to act as these laws command them, and to
see that others act in likewise.

And in addition to the abovesaid: **We do command** those persons
who by our leave are now discovering, that in the territory discovered
they make an estimation of the tributes and service that the Indians
should give, as vassals of the crown, and that said tribute be moderate,
so that they may bear it, taking account of the preservation of said Indians, and with said tribute, they shall go to the *comendero*, wherever he
may be, so that the Spaniards have no hand or ingress in the Indians,
nor power nor command whatsoever, nor shall they use or employ them
through *Naboria*[4] or in any other manner whatsoever, either large or
small, nor may they enjoy said tribute beyond that which the *Audiencia*

---

[4] In personal service; the word is adopted from the Tainos, for whom the *naborias*
were the subordinates of the cacique, as those "in service" at the royal courts of Europe
were subordinate to the nobles they served.

or governor may order for taking from them, and in all this, **We command** that we be informed of the quality of the land, and that this be put among the other matters in the letters-patent that are given said discoverers.

Many times it happens that persons who reside in the Indies come or send to plead with us that we grant them some things there, and because we have not the information here, whether of the quality of the person who so sues for our favour, and his merits and ability, or of the thing that is sought of us, judgement cannot be made to the satisfaction that one would desire: **And so We command** that said person shall declare in the *Audiencia*, there, that which we are asked to pass judgement upon, so that said *Audiencia* may inform itself both of the quality of the person and of the matter, and that it send said information, well closed, and sealed, with its opinion, to our Council of the Indies, so that with said information and opinion more light may be had of that which touches upon our service, and upon the judgement.

It is our will, and We do so command, that the Indians who at the present time are alive on the Islands of San Juan and Cuba and Hispaniola, now and for the time that it may please us, be not troubled or molested with tributes or other royal services, whether personal or mixed, more than are the Spaniards residing in said islands, and that they be allowed to rest, so that they may better multiply, and that they be instructed in the things of our holy Catholic faith, and for this, that they be given the number of religious persons that may be needed.

Said ordinances and matters contained in our letter, and each and every part of it, shall be communicated to each and every one of ye in those places and jurisdictions belonging to ourselves and under our Crown, and these things that we have ordered shall be observed and obeyed and performed and carried out with great diligence and special care, and eke be made by all subjects to be observed and obeyed and performed and carried out in every wise and manner, as contained in our letter, and against the tenor and form of the above-commanded, thou shalt not act or consent or pass over now or in any future time, or in any manner, under pain of that which we have commanded, and so that all the above-commanded and above-contained be better known, especially to the naturals of our Indies, in whose benefit and profit these things are ordered, we do command that this, our letter be printed in block letters and sent to all our Indies, to the religious persons who reside there and who take a hand in the instruction of said Indians, and that these things be translated into the language of the Indies so that they may better understand them and know what we have commanded, and that none disobey or allow to disobey, under pain of our mercy and one thousand gold *castellanos* for our purse to each person who might act in contrary, and we do further command that any person to whom our letter may be shown and who disobeys thee, that such person be brought before us in our Court, wherever we may be, from the day he disobeys thee to the space of one year thence, under said pain above. . . . Given in the city of Barcelona on this twentieth day of the month of November, in the year of our Saviour Jesus Christ one thousand five hundred forty-two,

I the King.

I Joan de Samano, Secretary of their Caesarean and Catholic Majesties, did make this to be written, upon their command.

Frater. H. Cardinalis Hispalensis

Doctor Guevara   Doctor Figueroa

Registered

Ochoa de Luyando, by Chancellor

Ochoa de Luyando

A Treatise on the Just Causes for War against the Indians

Juan Ginés de Sepúlveda (ca. 1490–1574), from Pozoblanco in Córdoba, certainly ranks among the distinguished jurists of his time. Educated at Alcalá and in Italy, he earned doctorates at Bologna in the early 1520s in both theology and law. He was a prolific writer and expert theologian. As a court insider in Spain, Sepúlveda spoke with a number of the returning distinguished conquistadors, including Hernán Cortés, and translated the multi-volume history of Gonzalo Fernández de Oviedo y Valdés (originally written in Castilian) into Latin. In opposing the position of Las Casas in the celebrated "debates" at Valladolid in 1550–1551, Sepúlveda relied on the Aristotelian concept of natural superiority reflected in the differential attributes of the parts of the body. Rational people, for him, were clearly superior to irrational people who violated natural laws. He considered the Spanish the most rational of Europeans, and therefore the indigenous populations of the Americas deserved their servitude at the hands of the Spanish.

Juan Ginés de Sepúlveda:
Tratado sobre las justas causas de la guerra contra los indios
A Treatise on the Just Causes for War against the Indians

. . . The second cause which justifies war against barbarians is that their sins, impieties, acts of wantonness, and sins of the flesh are so heinous and so abhorred by God, that offended principally with them, He destroyed all mortals with the exception of Noah and some few innocents with the universal Deluge. For those words of Holy Scripture, "The earth was corrupt before God, and the earth was filled with violence, and God looked upon the earth, and, behold, it was corrupt; for all flesh had corrupted his way upon the earth"[1] are explained in this way by a

---

[1] Gen. 6:11–2.

very ancient writer named Beroso: "They ate the flesh of men, they cast out children from the womb, and they lay carnally with their mothers, daughters, sisters, and with men and beasts." And he adds that for these crimes the universal flood did come. And the Holy Scripture itself plainly manifests[2] that it was for the sin of heinous wantonness that fire and brimstone did fall from the sky and destroy Sodom and Gomorra and all the region therearound and all the inhabitants of those cities, with the exception of Lot and some few just servants. And the Lord did insinuate to the Jews and inspire them that they should persecute the Canaanites, Amorites, and Perizzites with most severe and unstinting war, and exterminate them all, with their asses and their flocks.[3] And what is the reason for this condemnation but the crimes aforesaid, and principally the worship of false idols? All these crimes, the Lord abhors, as He has said to us, and for them He shall smite them down, and in another place he adds: "And if the people of the land do any ways hide their eyes from the man, when he giveth of his seed unto Molech, and kill him not: then I will set my face against that man, and against his family, and will cut him off, and all that go a whoring after him, to commit whoredom with Molech, from among their people. And the soul that turneth after such as have familiar spirits, and after wizards, to go a whoring after them, I will even set my face against that soul, and will cut him off from among his people."[4] And like unto these words, there are others, which may be read in *Deuteronomy*, in detestation of idols: "If thou shalt hear say in one of thy cities, which the Lord thy god hath given thee to dwell there, saying, Certain men, the children of Belial, are gone out from among you, and have withdrawn the inhabitants of their city, saying, Let us go and serve other gods, which ye have not known; then shalt thou enquire, and make search, and ask diligently; and, behold, if it be truth, and the thing certain, that such abomination is wrought among you; thou shalt surely smite the inhabitants of that city with the edge of the sword, destroying it utterly, and all that is therein, and the cattle thereof, with the edge of the sword."[5] And recalling this rigorous precept, Mathathias slew that man who approached the altar to make sacrifice to the false idols, as we read in the book of Machabees.[6]

---

[2] In, according to Sepúlveda, Genesis 19.

[3] Deut. 17:2–5; 18:10–2.

[4] Lev. 20:4–6.

[5] Deut. 13:12–5.

[6] 1 Mach. 2:23–4. These spellings of the book of Machabees and of Mathathias' name follow the "New Catholic Edition" of the Bible; other sources, such as Edgar J. Goodspeed's modern translation of the Apocrypha (New York: Vintage, 1959 [1938]), give the spellings as "Maccabees" and "Mattathias."

We may believe, then, that God has given great and exceedingly clear instructions respecting the destruction of these barbarians. Nor are there lacking exceedingly learned theologians who cleave to the fact that those words given against Jews who would prevaricate, or against the Canaanites, Amorites, and other peoples who worshipped false idols are not divine law alone, but natural law as well—and hence law not alone to the Jews but also to Christians—and those theologians do therefrom maintain that it is lawful not only to subject these barbarians, polluted with heinous acts of lasciviousness and the impious worship of false gods, to our dominion in order to bring them to spiritual health and the true religion by means of evangelical teaching, but also to castigate them with yet more severe war. And it appears that Saint Ciprian, citing that place in *Deuteronomy* and other similar places, would accord, for he adds this: "If before the coming of Christ these precepts concerning divine worship, and in reprobation of idolatry, were observed by men, how much more shall they be observed after the coming of Christ, when He has exhorted us, not alone with word but also with works?"

The True History of the Conquest of Mexico by Captain Bernal Díaz del Castillo

Bernal Díaz del Castillo (1492–1584) was born in Medina del Campo and died in Guatemala. Although he does not appear among those listed in Vilma Benso de Ferrer's Pasajeros a La Española 1492–1530 (Santo Domingo: Benso de Ferrer, 2000), Díaz del Castillo probably spent time on the island before serving with various commanders such as Pedro Arias de Avila, Diego de Velásquez, and Francisco de Córdoba, before joining Hernán Cortés' expedition to Mexico in 1519. On hearing of all the glory and reputation that Cortés had gathered, Díaz del Castillo decided in his old age in Guatemala to write an account of the conquest of Mexico as he remembered it. A remarkable account, it presents a poetic, highly insightful history that marvelously captures the zeitgeist of his age. The True History shows an exceptional appreciation for the local scene and its people, but nevertheless retains a powerful Hispanic point of view—albeit more from the perspective of the secular colonizers than from the clergy or the Crown.

The True History of the Conquest of Mexico, by Captain Bernal Díaz del Castillo, One of the Conquerors, Written in the Year 1568, translated from the original Spanish by Maurice Keatinge, Esq. (London, 1800)

Let the curious reader consider the number of cities of New Spain, which from *their* being so many, I will not detail; our ten bishoprics, not including the archbishopric of the noble city of Mexico, the three courts of royal audience, together with the succession of governors, archbishops, and bishops, our holy cathedrals and monasteries, Dominican, Franciscan, Mercenarian, and *Augustin*, our hospitals with the extensive remissions and pardons attached to them, and the Santa

Casa of our Lady of Guadeloupe with the holy miracles there performed every day, and let us give thanks to God, and to his blessed
mother our Lady, for giving us grace and support to conquer these
countries, where so much christianity is now established.

Let it be also remembered, that in Mexico there is a university
wherein are studied and learned grammar, theology, rhetoric, logic,
philosophy, and other sciences. There is also a printing press for books
both in Latin and Romance, and in this college they graduate as licen-
tiates and doctors; to which I might add many other instances to en-
hance the value of these countries, such as the mines of silver, and other
discoveries, whereby prosperity and grandeur redound to the mother
country. If all which I have now said does not suffice, let the wise and
learned read my history from beginning to end, and they will then confess, that there never existed in the world men who by bold atchieve-
ment have gained more for their Lord and King, than we the brave
conquerors; amongst the most valiant of whom I was considered as one,
and am the most ancient of all. I say again that I, —I myself, —I, am a
true conqueror: and the most ancient of all.

I will now propose a few questions by way of dialogue, with the immortal and illustrious goddess of Fame, who has seen, and proclaims
through the world, our manifold, great, and remarkable services, to
God, his Majesty and all Christendom, and cries with a loud voice, saying, that it is in justice and in reason, that we should have better estates
and situations than others who have not served his Majesty here or elsewhere. The goddess also enquires where are our palaces, and mansions,
adorned with distinguishing blazons, with sculptures of our coats of
arms, and monumental trophies of our heroic actions, in the same manner as those cavaliers have who served their king in Spain, our atchieve-
ments being no way inferior to theirs, but on the contrary of most
eminent merit, and not exceeded by any. The goddess of Fame also enquires for those conquerors who escaped from cruel deaths, and for the
tombs and monuments of those who fell.

To these questions I reply as follows, with much brevity. Oh excellent
and illustrious Fame! desired and sought for by the good and virtuous,
but shunned and hated by the malicious, why do you not exalt us as our
merits deserve? know, goddess, that of five hundred and fifty soldiers
who left the Island of Cuba with Cortés, at the moment that I am writing this history in the year one thousand five hundred and sixty eight no
more than five are living, the rest having been killed in the wars, sacrificed to idols, or died naturally. In answer to your questions concerning
their tombs and monuments, I tell you that their tombs are the maws of
cannibal Indians, who devoured their limbs, and of tigers, serpents, and

birds of prey, which feasted on their mangled bodies. Such were their sepulchres, and such their monuments! But to me it appears that the names of those ought to be written in letters of gold, who died so cruel a death, for the service of God and his Majesty, to give light to those who were in darkness, and to procure wealth which all men desire.

From Hernán Cortés
Cartas de relación

Hernán Cortés (1485–1547) was born in Medellín in Estremadura, Spain, and died near Seville. As a sickly child of the impoverished lower nobility, he attended the University of Salamanca for a short time but left without a degree. He went to Santo Domingo in 1504 where his fellow Estremeño (as those from Estremadura are called), Nicolás de Ovando, received him warmly. He went with Diego de Velásquez to subjugate Cuba, and while there married well and even served as alcalde (or mayor) of the newly established town of Santiago de Cuba while he searched for gold. Although there was not much gold in Cuba, Cortés struck it rich when (in 1519) he led an expedition to Mexico that overthrew the Aztec empire of Montezuma and found enormous amounts of gold and, later, silver. Although he was rewarded with the title of Marquis of the Valley of Oaxaca and given extensive authority, Cortés was never admitted to the inner circles at the Spanish court of Charles V, and indeed, much of the power of his offices was superseded by the appointment of a viceroy to New Spain in 1535. In his Cartas de relación, Cortés attempted to win favor at court by reminding the monarch of the great deeds accomplished by his servant. They demonstrate that, like Columbus, Cortés had remarkable powers of observation and a great eye for detail. In the writing of Cortés, much like that of Bernal Díaz del Castillo, there is pronounced admiration for the culture and society of the Aztecs. Their appreciation of the indigenous societies and cultures of the Americas did not betray the ethnocentricity of Juan Ginés de Sepúlveda.

This grand city of Temixtitan[1] is founded on this salt lake, and from Terra Firma to the body of that city, however one would enter it, is a distance of two leagues. It has four entrances, all of a broad way made by hand, and as wide as two horse-lances. As large as Sevilla and Córdoba is this city, and the streets of it, or the principal ones I mean, are very

---

[1] Tenochtitlán, the Aztec name for the City of Mexico.

broad and very straight, and some of these principal streets and all the others are half of earth, with the other half of water, on which the inhabitants travel with their *canoas*, and all the streets from one side to another open, and through that place the water runs from one to another, and in all these openings, some very wide, there are very wide bridges, with their beams very large, sturdy, and well-carven, and so broad that along many of them ten horsemen might pass abreast. And seeing that if the natives of this city took it upon them to enact some betrayal, they would have good means of doing so, the city being built in the way that I have said, and should the bridges at the entrances and egresses be taken down, they could well let us starve before we could come out onto land. After I entered into this city, I made great haste to build four brigantines, and I made them in very short time, so that they might put three hundred men back onto the land and carry horses whenever we might wish.

This city has many plazas, in which there is a constant market and much buying and selling. It has another plaza two times as large as the city of Salamanca, all fenced in with portals all around, in which every day over sixty thousand souls arrive, buying and selling, and in which there is every sort of merchandise that might be found in all the land, and commodities such as victuals, jewels of gold and silver, of lead, of brass, of copper, of tin, of gems, of bone, of mother-of-pearl, of cowries, and of feathers. Lime is sold there, and stone both trimmed and untrimmed, and adobe, and bricks, and divers kinds of wood, both dressed[2] and not. There is a street for game and fowl where every lineage of bird that is found upon the earth is sold, such as hens, partridges, quails, ducks, fly-catchers, garganeys, turtledoves, pigeons, little birds in reed cages, parrots, owls, eagles, falcons, hawks, and kestrels, and the skins, with the plumage and heads and beaks and claws, of some of these birds of prey are also sold.

They sell rabbits, hares, deer, and castrated small dogs that they raise for to eat. There is a street of herb-sellers, where one may find all the medicinal roots and herbs that grow upon the earth. There are houses like unto apothecary-shops, in which prepared pharmacies[3] are sold, both those that be drunk and unguents and plasters. There are houses like unto barbers, where heads are washed and shorn. There are houses where for a certain price one may eat and drink. There are men like those called *bearers*, which bear heavy loads. There is a great lot of fire-

---

[2] Trimmed, smoothed, the bark taken off, etc.

[3] I.e., medicines and remedies.

wood, charcoal, clay braziers, and mats of many kinds that they use for beds, and others, not so thick, to sit upon and to lay like carpets upon the parlors and bedchambers. There are all manner of greenstuffs that can be found, especially onions, leeks, garlic, watercress and other like plants, borage, sorrel, and sour dock and oyster plant, as they call them. There are fruits of many kinds, amongst which one finds cherries, and plums that much resemble those of Spain. They sell honey and wax from bees and honey also from maize plants, which is as sweet as sugar, and the sweet sap of some plants which on the other islands are called magüey, which is infinitely better than grapesugar or even the honey from bees, and from these plants they do make both sugar and wine, and sell those things as well. For sale are many kinds of threads spun from cotton, and of all colours, in their skeins, laid out in such great quantity that they resemble the silk customs-house at Granada, though if truth be told, the market in this place is much greater even than ours. They sell colours for painters, as many as one might hope to find in Spain, and of such excellent hues as one could desire. They sell deer hides with the hair on and without it, some dyed white and also other colours. They sell crockery of every sort, of very fine quality, large oil vessels, or for water, and also small ones, and jars and pitchers, pots, bricks and a very infinite number of shapes and kinds, all of singular clay, all—or the most of them—put in the kiln and fired, and painted.

They sell much maize, both in the grain and as bread, and this, I daresay, both in grain and taste, outstrips that of all the other islands and the rest of Terra Firma. They sell pasties of birds and fish, and fish put up other ways as well—fresh and dried, raw and stewed. They sell hens' eggs and goose eggs and the eggs of all the other fowl that I have said above, in great quantity; and they sell eggs cooked up to eat. Finally, in these markets they sell all manner of things that may be found in all the land, which in addition to those things I have said, are so many, and of such quality, that on account of the number of them and because my memory begins to fail me, and yet more on account of not knowing the names of them all, I shall say no more. Each kind of good has its own street, in which it is sold, and no other merchandise of any kind is to be found there, and in this, they have much order. All things are sold by count and measure, except that until now I have not seen them sell any thing at all by weight.

In this great plaza there is a great house, like unto a courthouse or the court itself, where ten or twelve persons are always sitting, and these are the judges, who hear all the cases and matters that occur in that market, and they order criminals punished. And in that market there be other persons who walk about constantly amongst the people, looking at

what is being sold and the measures by which it be measured, and some
who cheat have been seen arrested.

There are, in this great city, many mosques or houses of their idols,
very beautiful buildings, in certain parts and neighborhoods of the city,
and in the principal of these houses there are religious persons of their
sect who reside constantly in them, and for these buildings, in addition
to the houses where they have their idols, there are good apartments. All
these religious men dress in black, and they never cut their hair nor
comb it, from the time they enter the religion until they leave it, and all
the sons of the principal persons, both lords and honest commoners, are
in those worships and habits from the age of seven or eight until they are
taken from it to marry, and this occurs most in the first-born who are to
inherit the house, than in the others. They have not access to women,
nor does any woman enter into these houses of religion. They observe
abstinence in the eating of certain delicacies, and more in some times
of the year than in others, and of these mosques there is one that is the
principal one, and there is no human tongue that can tell the grandeur
and particularities of it, because it is so great that within it, which is all
walled about with a very high wall, one could very well put a town of
five hundred persons. Within this circuit, all around, there be very fine
dwellings in which there are large halls and rooms and corridors in
which the religious men that are there reside. There are some forty towers, very high and finely worked, and the largest has fifty steps to reach
the tower, and the most principal of these is higher than the tower of the
cathedral in Sevilla. They are so well carven, in both stone and wood,
that they could not be better worked or carven anywhere, for all the
stonework inside the chapels where they have their idols is of great
imagining and elaborate carving, and the woodwork is all of Masonic
signs and well painted with monsters and other figures and labours. All
of these towers are the burial places of their lords, and eke the chapels
where each one is dedicated to its idol, which they do worship.

There are three halls within this great mosque where the principal
idols are, and they are of marvellous greatness and height, and of great
carving and graven[4] figures, in both stonework and woodwork, and
within these halls there are eke other chapels, and the doors by which
one enters them are very low, and they themselves have no light whatever, and therein, there be but religious men, and not all, and within
these chambers are the statues and figures of the idols, although, as I
have said, without there are also many. The most principal of these

---

[4] Sculpted.

idols, and those in whom these people put most faith and belief, I commanded to be tumbled from their seats and thrown down the stairs, and I commanded that those chapels where they had had them be cleaned, because all were filled with the blood that they sacrifice, and I put in them images of Our Lady and other saints, and the aforesaid Mutezuma and the natives did grieve much at this. First they told me that I must not do it, because if it were known by the communities they would rise against me, because they believed that those idols gave them all temporal and worldly goods, and if they should be allowed to be treated ill, they would grow angry and give naught, and they would make the fruit of the earth to rot, and the people would die of hunger. I had them understand by the tongues[5] how deceived they were in having hope from those idols, that were made by their own hands, and of unclean things, and I had them know that there was but one God, the universal Lord of all, who had created the heavens and the earth and all things upon it, and had made them and us, and that He was without beginning and immortal, and that He was to be adored and believed, and not any other creature or thing whatever, and I told them all other things that I could in this matter, to turn them from their idolatries and bring them to the knowledge of God our Lord. And all, especially said Mutezuma, answered that they had told me that they were not natives of this land, and that it had been many long years that their predecessors had come here, and that they believed that they might be mistaken in some of the things that they took for belief, by cause of the long time that had passed since they departed their native land, and that I, more newly come, might know things that they should hold in belief better than they themselves; and that I should tell them and have them to understand it, and that they would do what I told them, which was best. And Mutezuma and many of the principal men of that city stayed with me until the idols had been taken away and the chapels cleaned and the new images put in their places, and all with seeming joy, and I forbade them from killing creatures for the idols, as they had wont to do, because not only was it abominable in the sight of God, but our holy majesty had forbade it in his laws, and had ordered that he who killed be likewise killed. And from that time forward they did leave off sacrificing as they had wont to do, and in all the time I was in that city, never was any creature seen killed or sacrificed.

---

[5] The interpreters that Cortés had, among them the famous "Doña Marina," or Malinche.

The statues and bodies of the idols in which these people believe are of much greater stature than the body of a large man. They are made of the paste of all the seeds and grains[6] that they do eat, ground and mixed one with another, and they do knead them up with the blood of the hearts of human bodies, whose breasts they open, alive, and take out the heart, and with that blood that comes out with it, they knead up that flour, and so they make as much quantity as they require for those great statues. And also, after these statues are made, they offer them more hearts, which they sacrifice in the same way, and they smear their faces with the blood. And each thing has its idol dedicated to it, in the manner of the Gentiles who in ancient times worshipped their gods in that way. So that to ask a favor in war they have one idol, and for their crops another, and likewise for each thing that they wish or desire to be done well, they have their idols, whom they honor and serve.

There are in this great city many very fine and very large houses, and the cause for having so many principal houses is that all the lords of the land, vassals of said Mutezuma, have their houses in this city, and reside in it for a certain time each year, and besides this there are many rich citizens who likewise have fine houses. All of them have, besides very large, fine chambers and apartments,[7] very gracious gardens of flowers of many kinds, both in the lower chambers and the upper. Along the causeway that enters this great city come two channels made of masonry and mortar, as broad as two paces each, and as high as one *estado*, and through one of them comes a stream of very delicious sweet water, as thick as a man's body, which furnishes the most of the city, and which all persons do take from, and drink. The other channel, which is empty, is for when they desire to clean the other channel, for they turn the water into this one while the other is a-cleaning, and because the water must pass across bridges, because of the streambeds through which the salt water must pass, they turn the sweet water into channels as thick as an ox and of the length of those bridges, and so the entire city may be served.

They sell this water in their *canoas*, as they call their little boats, in all the streets, and the way they take it from the channel is that the *canoas* are rowed under the bridges across which the channels run, and on those bridges there are men, up above there, who fill the *canoas*, and they are paid for their work. At all the entrances to the city, and in the parts where the *canoas* are unloaded, which is where the most of the

---

[6] Beans and peas.
[7] Rooms, chambers.

goods for maintaining the city enter it, there are huts where persons are put as guards, and they receive *certum quid* for each thing that enters. This, I know not if it go to the lord or if it be for the city, for until now I have not learned that, but I do think that it be for the lord, for in other markets in other provinces that tax has been seen to be for the lord of them. In all the markets and public places of this city, there are, every day, many persons, workers, and masters of all trades and occupations, awaiting the man that might hire them for their labour.

The people of this city are more cleanly and exquisite in their dress and comportment than any other nations of these provinces and cities, for because this lord Mutezuma is always near, and all the lords his vassals are about the city, there is in all things a measure and a polity. And so as not to be more prolix in the telling of the things of this great city, although I would not end so shortly, I would say no more but that in these people's comportment and service there is a manner nigh about the life in Spain itself, and with such great concert and order as there, and that considering this people to be so barbaric and so far from the knowledge of God and communication with other nations of reason,[8] it is remarkable to see the order and measure that they have in all things.

Respecting the service of Mutezuma and the admirable things of state and greatness that he possessed, there is so much to write that I do vow to Your Highness that I know not where to begin to speak of even a part of them. For as I have said, what grander thing might there be than a barbaric lord such as this who yet had counterfeits of gold and silver and gems and feathers, all the things under heaven that you yourself have in your kingdom, so naturally contrived of gold and silver that there is no silversmith in the world that might do it better, and as for the precious gems, there is not intelligence sufficient to understand with what instruments they have so skillfully wrought them, and as for the feathers, there is neither wax nor any lace that can be done so wonderfully. The lands over which this Mutezuma holds sway, I have not been able to discover how wide they spread, because nowhere, two hundred leagues from one end to the other of this great city, might he send his messengers that his word be not obeyed, save in some of the provinces in the midst of these lands with which he was at war. But as for that which he did hold sway over, and that I could grasp, his kingdom was nigh as large as all of Spain, because as much as sixty leagues from this place Putunchán, which is the Grijalva River, he sent messengers to say

---

[8] I.e., rational nations; the natives of the New World were sometimes not seen to be rational creatures.

that the natives of a city they call Cumatán should become vassals of
your majesty, and from this great city to that one, it is two hundred
twenty leagues. . . . All the other lords of these lands and provinces, and
especially of certain regions, resided, as I have said, much of the year in
that great city, and all, or most, had their first-born sons in the service of
said Mutezuma.

In all the lands under these particular lords, Mutezuma had armies,
and his people, and his governors and collectors of the taxes and rents
that each province did give him, and there was good accounting of what
each was to give, for they have characters and figures written on paper
that they make, so that they may know. Each of these provinces served
with its particular kind of services, so that into this Mutezuma's power
came whatever sorts of things that each province might possess. He was
so feared by all, both present and absent, that there was never a prince
of this world more feared. He had, both within the city and without,
many houses of pleasure, and each one in its manner of pastime, as well
carven as might be imagined, and everything that might be required by
a great prince and lord. He had within the city his dwelling houses, and
so wondrous were they that it would seem to me almost impossible to
tell the fineness and excellence of them, and for that reason I will not
tarry to say more of them than that in Spain, there is not their like.

He had one house somewhat less fine than this, wherein he had a
most handsome garden with certain rooms up on the roof that did hang
out over it, and the marbles and tiles in these apartments were of fine-
wrought jasper. In this house there were dwelling-places for two very
great princes, with all their service. And this house did have ten ponds
of water, in which all the kinds of water birds and water fowls that are
found in these lands were kept, and many and divers they are, and all
domestic. And for the fowl that are born and live upon the sea, there
were pools of salt water, and for those of the rivers, lakes of sweet water,
which they did empty from time to time, to clean, and then filled again
from their channels, and each kind of bird was given that food that was
native to it, and that it had nourished itself on in the field. Thus, those
that ate fish were given fish, and those that ate worms were given
worms, and those that ate maize were given maize, and those that ate
other smaller seeds, likewise. And I do vow to Your Highness that the
birds that ate naught but fish were given ten *arrobas* of fish each day,
caught in salt water. To care for these fowl there were three hundred
men, who no other thing attended to. There were other men whose
only task was to cure the birds that became sick or ailing. Above each
pool and tank for these birds there were their corridors and outlooks, all

very finely carven, where said Mutezuma came to recreate,[9] and see them. And in this house he had a room in which he had men and women and children that were white from birth, in their countenances and bodies and hair and brows and lashes. He had another very handsome house wherein he had a large patio tiled with most refined tiles, all made in the semblance of a chess board, and the houses were a full *estado* and a half deep, and as large as six paces square, and the half of the basement of one of these houses was covered with tiles, and the half that was not covered had a net of woven withes, very well crafted, above it, and in each of these houses there was a bird of prey, commencing with the kestrel to the eagle, every bird that is found in Spain and many kinds, yet stranger, that are not. And of each of these bird's kind there were many, and on the roof of each of these houses there was a post like a falcon perch, and another under the net of withes, and upon one they would perch at night or when there was rain, and on the other they might go out into the sun and air to regain their health. And all these birds were given hens to eat every day, and no other food. In this house there were certain large, very low[-ceilinged] rooms, all filled with cages of thick wood, well crafted and strongly set, and in all, or most, of them there were lions, tigers, wolves, foxes, and cats of all kinds, and many of each kind, and they, also, were given all the hens that they might require. And for these animals and birds there were another three hundred men charged with their keeping.

He had another house in which he had many monstrous men and women, dwarves, hunchbacks, and twisted, and others with other deformities, and each kind of monster in a room of its own, and there were also for these creatures, persons to watch over and care for them, and the other things of pleasure that he had in his city I will not name, for they are many and of many kinds. . . .

---

[9] Rest, relax, take recreation.

Table of Weights and Measures
Used in the Text

arroba	25 pounds (0.25 quintal)
carga	Variable, but always a dry measure, the *carga* was used sometimes for grains, sometimes for such commodities as wood, and was equal in some places to approximately 3 *fanegas*, in others to about 4, i.e., 150–200 dry liters, or about 5 to 7 bushels
castellano	A coin in use since more than a hundred years earlier, equivalent to 4.6 grams, or 0.16 ounce; by today's price of gold, approximately US$40; not minted after 1497 and thus considered by numismatists a "medieval" unit of currency
estado	7 feet (more or less—not a particularly exact measurement); also a surface measure of about 49 square feet
fanega	55.5 liters; about 1.5 bushels (1 bushel ~ 35–36 liters)
league (area)	3,105.5 hectares; almost 12 square miles, or 7,674 acres
league (length)	The Spanish, not English, measurement; equal to 20,000 feet, approximately 3.78 miles
quintal	100 pounds
vara	33 inches (roughly 1 yard)

Glossary of Political and Military Terms Used in the Text

Audiencia Real   A royal court of justice, acting as the representative of the monarchy to settle disputes in the New World. Its members were appointed by the monarch, and because the monarch was the supreme authority, the monarchy's representative was supreme as well, and had to be respected. Those who failed to show respect for the *Audiencia Real*, or who failed to obey its rulings, were considered traitors to the crown (see the end of "On the Province and Kingdom of Guatimala," and also Las Casas' "Testament" in the last pages of the text for clear cases of such treason). Thus, the coming of an *Audiencia Real* to the New World was (at least potentially, if never actually) a great threat to the looters and pillagers, who for years had flouted every law handed down to control them. This institution originated in ancient Castile.

comendero   Also *encomendero*; the holder of an *encomienda* (see below).

encomendado   Used here in the sense of "land [i.e., not the inhabitants] that had been given to colonists as an *encomienda*" (see below); in other contexts, this word might have several meanings within the military/political structure.

encomendero   The holder of an *encomienda* (see below).

encomienda   A semifeudal system of labor organization that had been traditional in Spain. Because the crown had forbidden Columbus to enslave the Indians, a labor "crisis" ensued; there was no way to work the land or till the fields for food *and* work the mines for gold. Nicolás de Ovando, who followed Columbus as governor of Hispaniola, decided to implement the *encomienda*, which "assigned" or "allotted" to the Spanish "settlers" (the idea of settlement being a convenient fiction for the gold-seekers and looters) a certain area of land and gave the *encomendero* the right to employ the indigenous people who lived on that land to work it and also to perform other functions (such as, not surprisingly, to find him gold), with the condition that the workers be well fed and cared for, be paid for their services, and be instructed in the

Catholic faith. (The word *encomendar* (v.)/*encomienda* (n.) indicates that something or someone is put in one's care for guardianship or safekeeping.) Obviously these conditions were seldom met, and the *encomienda* system was in fact no better than slavery. One aspect of the *encomienda* needs to be noted, and that is that unlike feudal assignments of land and peasants, the assignment of an *encomienda* was not hereditary, could not be inherited; the Spanish crown did not want to create a class of feudal lords who might challenge monarchic authority.

entrada   When Spaniards sailed from Spain for the Indies or later for other parts of the New World, the leader of an expedition (the *adelantado*) would carry a *capitulación*, what was called in the English-speaking world a "letter-patent," or grant, permit, or contract that gave the *adelantado* permission to "enter" (*entrar*) or "open" certain areas for the crown. When the party arrived in the New World, then, the leader would exercise these permissions by "making *entradas*" into the country. Basically, when a group of Spaniards went into previously "unexplored" (by them, of course) or "unopened" territory, they made their "entrance" (*entrada*) into that territory not by hacking their way through the jungle but rather by officially "claiming" it, with certain ritual accompaniments, for the crown and the church. Often, after 1512, this meant reading the *requerimiento* (see below) to the indigenous peoples that they encountered.

oidores   (sing. *oidor*) In the New World, the officials of a settlement, similar perhaps to "city councilmen" today, though with somewhat more power to "hear" (the root meaning of the word) cases and deliver justice; in Spain, from whence the title originates, these officials were magistrates of the courts or tribunals.

repartimiento   The *repartimiento* is very similar to the *encomienda*. It was instituted on Hispaniola by Columbus as a way of dealing with the labor shortage (producing food and mining for gold); he assigned to the "settlers" a certain number of indigenous people, who were expected to perform labor for the Spaniards. *Repartimiento* means "distribution" or "parceling-out," and basically that is what Columbus did: he parceled out the native-born peoples that they lived among to the Spaniards. No land was necessarily attached to this assignment; only "Indians" were distributed. Due to desertion and death among the indigenes, however, this system collapsed.

requerimiento   As the text indicates, this was a text, read to the native-born peoples, which notified them of the existence of the Catholic Church and the king (or king and queen) of Spain and urged them to pay those institutions fealty. This action stemmed from the monarchy's belief that it was unlawful to wage war on "discovered" peoples unless those peoples were first given the opportunity to come peacefully into the fold; once they had explicitly rejected the terms of the *requerimiento* and become either rebels or reprobates, they could be "conquered" or "pacified" and thereafter made slaves. (This is the notion of "just war" that the text refers to passim.) The *requerimiento* was instituted in 1512 as a way of controlling slave hunting and/or wholesale slaughter of unsuspecting indigenous peoples. (The *requerimiento* was often a legalism; as Las Casas indicates, it was sometimes read "to" the native peoples out of their earshot or while they were asleep; it was also, of course, in Spanish, or sometimes Latin, which no native peoples would have understood.)

Visitadores   The local investigative government officials established by the Laws of Burgos (1512–1513) for Hispaniola and Puerto Rico and extended throughout the Spanish American empire.

Index